Men-at-Arms • 202

Modern African Wars (2)

Angola and Mozambique 1961–74

P Abbott & M Rodrigues • Illustrated by R Volstad
Series editor Martin Windrow

First published in Great Britain in 1988 by Osprey Publishing,
Midland House, West Way, Botley, Oxford OX2 0PH, UK
44-02 23rd St, Suite 219, Long Island City, NY 11101, USA
E-mail: info@ospreypublishing.com

© 1988 Osprey Publishing Ltd.

All rights reserved. Apart from any fair dealing for the purpose of private study, research, criticism or review, as permitted under the Copyright, Designs and Patents Act, 1988, no part of this publication may be reproduced, stored in a retrieval system, or transmitted in any form or by any means, electronic, electrical, chemical, mechanical, optical, photocopying, recording or otherwise, without the prior written permission of the copyright owner. Inquiries should be addressed to the Publishers.

Transferred to digital print on demand 2007

First published 1988
4th impression 2005

Printed and bound in Great Britain

A CIP catalogue record for this book is available from the British Library

ISBN: 978 0 85045 843 5

Editorial by Martin Windrow
Index by Sandra Shotter

FSC
MIX
Paper from responsible sources
FSC® C013604

FOR A CATALOGUE OF ALL BOOKS PUBLISHED BY OSPREY MILITARY AND AVIATION PLEASE CONTACT:

Osprey Direct, c/o Random House Distribution Center,
400 Hahn Road, Westminster, MD 21157
Email: uscustomerservice@ospreypublishing.com

Osprey Direct, The Book Service Ltd, Distribution Centre,
Colchester Road, Frating Green, Colchester, Essex, CO7 7DW
E-mail: customerservice@ospreypublishing.com

www.ospreypublishing.com

Angola and Moçambique 1961-74

Preface

Portugal is a small country, but for many years it possessed the world's third largest empire; and its armed forces deserve to be better known than they are in the English-speaking world. The problem is that although the Portuguese sources are extensive, they are (quite naturally) housed in Portugal itself and written in Portuguese, which makes them relatively inaccessible to outsiders. Fortunately, the British co-author was able to meet a Portuguese colleague who was not only an authority on Portuguese military history and uniforms, but who had also served in Moçambique himself. A collaborative venture seemed the best way of providing the kind of 'hard' information about Portuguese weapons, organisation, uniforms and insignia that has been lacking until now. Even more fortunately, the Portuguese authorities raised no objection, and we are happy to acknowledge the generous assistance provided in particular by the Portuguese Army and Air Force.

It might be argued that the use of Portuguese sources carries with it some risk of prejudice against the African Liberation Movements. In fact, the generation which welcomed the Portuguese coup of April 1974 had already concluded that the Africans deserved their independence, and the hand-over in Angola, Guiné and Moçambique was generally concluded in a friendly and co-operative spirit. The Africans themselves always maintained that their struggle was against the Portuguese system rather

African troops on parade shortly before the outbreak of the war. They carry Mauser rifles, and wear leather equipment. In parade dress, whites wore either a slouch hat or steel helmet.

than the Portuguese people, and subsequent relations between Portugal and her one-time overseas provinces have remained good. We would not want to disparage either the aims or the achievements of the Liberation Movements in any way, and wish to pay tribute to the heroism and sacrifice shown by combatants of both sides.

Portugal's African Empire

Portugal was both the first and the last of the great European colonial powers. The discoveries inspired by Henry the Navigator in the 15th and early 16th centuries gave her an immense empire stretching from Brazil in the West to Macau in the Far East. Inevitably, many of these possessions were lost in the centuries which followed, but in 1960 the Portuguese flag still flew over vast expanses of territory in East, West and Southern Africa. It continued to fly there while the other European imperial powers were busy granting independence to their African colonies; and it was not until 1974–75 that it finally came down, ending some five centuries of involvement with Africa.

This is not the place to discuss Portuguese colonial policy in detail, but some of its salient features need to be noted in order to understand the background to the African Liberation Wars. Firstly, from 1951 onwards, official Portuguese doctrine was that the overseas territories were not 'colonies' at all, but integral parts of Portugal. These 'overseas provinces' had special laws suited to their particular level of development, but they were ruled from Lisbon and formed part of a Portuguese-speaking and strongly Christian 'political and spiritual community'. This was the 'New State' created by Dr Salazar, the effective ruler of Portugal from 1928 until 1968. Dr Salazar always denied that this was totalitarian, but it was unquestionably right wing and authoritarian. There was a National Assembly, but it had little power; and any organised opposition was suppressed by the regime's secret police, the *Policia Internacional de Defesa do Estado*, known as 'PIDE'.

Among the most important of the special laws for the overseas provinces were those dealing with the

An African unit, late 1950s: note the officers' closed collar tunics and combat boots, and the leather belts and pouches for the FPB sub-machine gun.

status of their inhabitants. The ultimate Portuguese goal was *assimilação uniformizadora* (equal assimilation for whites and blacks alike), but it was recognised that for the time being the majority of the inhabitants of the African provinces retained their own customs, languages and religions. Consequently the population was divided into *indígenas* (natives) and *não-indígenas*, a category which included white settlers, *mestiços* (half-castes) and *assimilados*. The latter were Africans who had learned Portuguese, accepted Christianity, shown that they could provide for themselves and their families and, finally, signed a declaration of loyalty. In effect, they were 'black Portuguese', entitled to all the privileges and liabilities of Portuguese citizenship.

The Portuguese prided themselves on their racial tolerance, and to a large extent this claim was justified. As early as 1684 the government had decreed that there should be no discrimination between whites, *mestiços* and free negroes within the Angolan army, and similar 'colour-blind' decrees

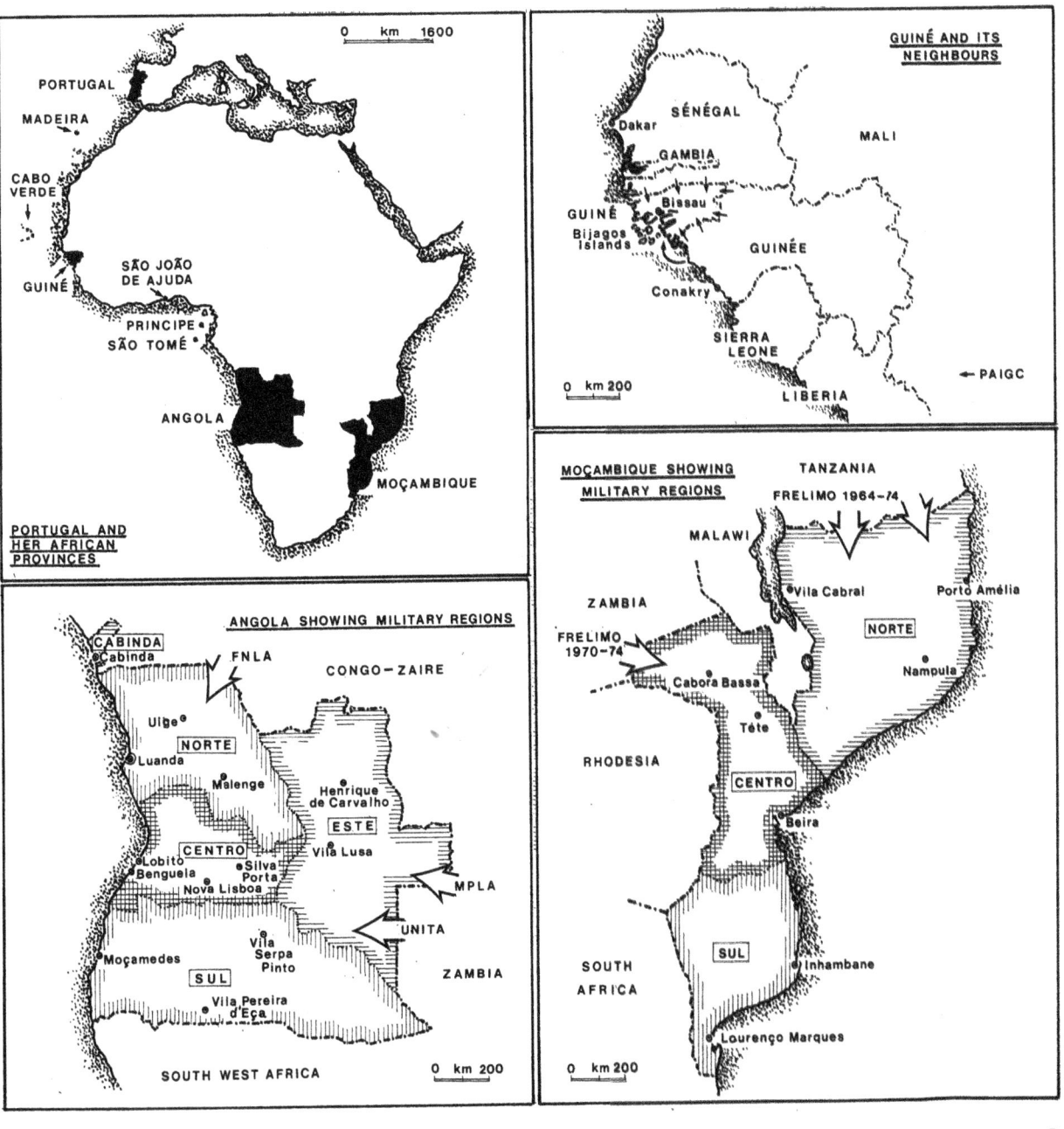

Black soldiers and white NCOs of an African unit, c.1960. The two white NCOs are armed with Steyr m/942 sub-machine guns, fitted with bayonets in accordance with contemporary Portuguese practice. Note the differences in uniform.

were promulgated during the 18th century. During the 19th century the half-caste Geraldo Victor (son of an Italian father and Angolan mother) became a general and a hero of the colonial wars. Later, travellers familiar with other colonial societies were often surprised to see whites cheerfully performing menial jobs for assimilated blacks in cities such as Luanda.

Like all colonial powers, Portugal expected her overseas provinces to raise at least some of the revenue needed to pay for their administration. This was particularly important for Portugal, because in spite of Dr Salazar's undoubted achievements she remained relatively poor. However, it meant that the *indígenas* were required to provide compulsory contract labour and had to comply with measures such as the forced cultivation of cash crops. Other colonial powers had passed similar laws during their early days, but only Portugal retained them into the 1950s. This problem was aggravated by the arrival of many thousands of Portuguese immigrants who arrived in Angola and Moçambique under the government's *colonato* schemes and who were dependent on the continued provision of forced labour. Personal relationships between black and white remained surprisingly good, but the system as a whole was bitterly resented by the local Africans, and provided fertile ground for nationalist exploitation.

Although the Portuguese authorities tried to insulate the overseas territories from any knowledge of the decolonisation process elsewhere, it was a hopeless task. The educated *mestiços* and *assimilados* were well aware of what was happening in other territories. They saw a series of British and French colonies win their independence during the later 1950s. They watched events in the Congo with special interest, for although the initial Belgian attitude had been very similar to the Portuguese one, events had shown how quickly a colonial power could be persuaded to change its mind and withdraw. They were encouraged by the fact that the Portuguese territories had begun to find themselves surrounded, not by other colonies, but by newly independent states whose governments were sympathetic to the cause of African nationalism. It seemed that their time had come.

The spread of decolonisation however, brought about no changes in Portuguese attitudes or policies. The official view remained that the overseas provinces were integral parts of the Portuguese state, and that what went on there was an internal matter, of no concern to the United Nations, whose expanding anti-colonial bloc became increasingly critical.

It was not possible to ignore the outside world completely, but the Portuguese did their best. In 1960 the French colony of Dahomey received its independence. Located within its small coastal town of Ajuda was perhaps the smallest colonial possession in the world, an old Portuguese fort with a garrison consisting of one Portuguese officer (who acted as the governor) and a few native soldiers. It was known grandly as 'the Portuguese territory of São João de Ajuda'. The new Dahomean government made a number of attempts to persuade the Portuguese to hand over the fort, but the Portuguese ignored them all. Finally, in 1961, the Dahomeans issued an ultimatum. Just before it expired, the Portuguese governor set fire to his residency and left for the airport to the accompaniment of full military honours. In subsequent handbooks on their African possessions the Portuguese included São João de Ajuda with the terse comment 'temporarily under enemy occupation'.

This attitude typified the Portuguese approach in their other and larger mainland territories. Other colonial powers might cut and run, but the Portuguese had been in Africa for 500 years. They had experienced revolts and even invasions before, and had always won through in the end. It was to be 13 long years before they realised that this time it was different.

The Liberation Movements

Apart from Fort São João, Portugal's African possessions consisted of the Cabo Verde Islands, lying off the extreme west coast and inhabited mainly by *mestiços*; the coffee-growing islands of São Tomé e Principe in the Gulf of Guinea; Portuguese Guiné, a swampy and unhealthy expanse situated between the ex-French colonies of Sénégal and Guinée (Conakry); Moçambique on the south-east coast; and Angola, the largest and potentially the richest of them all. The islands played little or no part in the liberation struggles because the Portuguese Navy was able to prevent the importation of arms and equipment. With the loss of São João, therefore, the story is confined to the three mainland territories of Angola, Guiné and Moçambique.

Each of the three mainland territories produced its own crop of liberation movements. The struggle against the Portuguese unfolded in different ways in the three territories, at different speeds and with varying degrees of success. However, all the movements had features in common. Their leaders were generally *mestiços* or *assimilados* who had studied in Lisbon and Paris and had become infected with nationalist ideas. Most were drawn towards Communism because Portugal's democratic opposition movement preferred to postpone discussion of colonial questions until after Dr Salazar's regime had been overthrown, and the Communists were the only Portuguese opposition party to come out in support of self-determination for the overseas provinces. Most knew each other

This sketch, based on an official Portuguese drawing, shows the *Auto-Metralhadora-Daimler 4 × 4 Mod.F/64*—in fact, the familiar Daimler Dingo scout car of the Second World War, with an additional turret-like structure (vaguely reminiscent of the turret of the Daimler Armoured Car) added to the superstructure, and the original gun-port faired over. According to the accompanying text in the Portuguese source, it had no fixed armament, but was armed at opportunity with light automatic weapons such as Madsens, Dreyses, FNs or G-3s. It was one of the types used by the independent reconnaissance platoons, along with the French Panhard AML-90 series, mainly for convoy work.

A black Commando officer decorated for valour, 1970. This photograph shows the 1963 pattern combat dress. At this period the Commando beret was brown, though this was later changed to the same crimson as the neckerchief.

through membership of Lisbon's Centre for African Studies or the clandestine Centre of Marxist Studies. Once armed struggle had begun, they continued to swap information and views through CONCP (the Algiers-based Conference of Nationalist Organisations in the Portuguese Colonies).

Not all the organisations were Marxist, but the Marxist groups were unquestionably the most successful. It is tempting to think that this was because they were supported by socialist states such as Guinée (Conakry) and Tanzania and received arms and equipment from Russia and China, but this is not entirely true. Sénégal, which was far from being a socialist state, supported several non-Marxist Guinéan groups; and Angola's FNLA had the advantages of Western finance as well as a friendly and non-Marxist Congolese government. The real truth seems to be that the Marxists paid more attention to political indoctrination and tried hard to enforce on their troops a discipline based on Mao's famous 'Three Rules and Eight Remarks'. They subordinated their military wings to the party and adopted the principle of collective leadership (though this did not prevent them from being dominated by powerful personalities like Guiné's Amilcar Cabral or Moçambique's Eduardo Mondlane). They opposed tribalism, even though many of their followers found this ideal difficult to accept in practice. They opposed racism, too, claiming that they were fighting the Portuguese political and colonial system but not the Portuguese people.

However, they were not monolithic. Like nationalist movements everywhere, they experienced policy disputes and even purges. Angola was to become a classic example of what could happen when nationalists fell out among themselves; but Moçambique's FRELIMO was also riven by disagreements, and the killing of its leader Mondlane seems to have been at least partly the work of the internal opposition. Guiné's PAIGC had its internal divisions, too, and its leader Cabral was certainly assassinated by a dissident from his own party.

We must now turn to a consideration of the individual liberation movements. Unfortunately, but inescapably, any study of modern African political movements involves a veritable 'alphabet soup' of initials. This can be confusing, but there is really no alternative.

Angola

The war began in Angola in 1961. There were already two rival nationalist movements, the UPA (later the *Frente Nacional de Libertação de Angola* or FNLA), and the *Movimento Popular de Libertação de Angola* or MPLA. The former had begun life as a nationalist organisation for the important Kongo people, who straddled the border between Angola and the Belgian Congo. When the Congo became independent in 1960, its government began to give the UPA's leader Holden Roberto practical assistance, including permission to set up a radio station and a training camp.

The MPLA, on the other hand, was very much a movement of radical intellectuals, with its main strength divided between the urbanised Angolans and the Ovimbundu people. It had been badly hurt by successive waves of arrests carried out by PIDE during 1959 and 1960, including that of its subsequent leader Dr Agostinho Neto; he later escaped from preventive detention in Portugal and joined his remaining colleagues in exile. More junior MPLA militants had then incited riots in Luanda which the Portuguese authorities put down without much difficulty, leaving the party in even greater disarray.

Meanwhile, disaffection over the enforced growing of cotton had led to a spontaneous peasant rising in early 1961. No sooner had this been suppressed than the Kongo in the north rose in revolt, massacring Europeans and *assimilados*. This rising was inspired by the UPA. It was put down by the Portuguese military and settler militia with considerable severity, and the UPA survivors fled across the Congolese border, apart from a remnant who took refuge in the hilly and heavily forested Dembos area north of Luanda—a traditional refuge for insurgents.

Despite this setback, the UPA (soon renamed FNLA) was still the stronger organisation. In addition to Congolese and Algerian support it also received covert supplies of funds and arms from the Americans, who were anxious to encourage non-Communist African nationalist movements as a counter-weight to the Marxists. The FNLA was thus able to build up a substantial force in its Congolese sanctuary. Roberto showed little interest in sending these men back into Angola, preferring to wait for a more propitious moment when his regulars would be able to hold the balance of power. However, much of the money he received seems to have been diverted into business ventures, and the movement's *Exército de Libertação Nacional de Angola* (ELNA) remained at a strength of some 6,200 men, stationed in Congo/Zaire and armed with light infantry weapons. These were mostly of the Soviet pattern and included SKS carbines, AK-47s and RPG rocket launchers. A few small groups launched raids across the northern frontier, and later a few patrols entered Eastern Angola from Kolwezi, but most of the men remained idle in their Kinkuzu camp. This policy sapped their morale, and in 1972 they mutinied. The Zairean army restored order and took over training; but although ELNA was able to mount an impressive parade on the eve of Angolan independence, its unimpressive performance in the subsequent civil war showed that the reorganisation had had little effect.

The MPLA recovered slowly from its initial setbacks, and it was not until 1965–66 that it began to replace the FNLA as the main resistance movement. It suffered from the hostility of the FNLA, and since Roberto was President Mobuto's brother-in-law he was able to persuade him not to grant his rivals bases on Congolese territory. The closest the MPLA leadership could get to Angola in

A parade during the early 1970s. Note the company banner bearing the well known 'Saint'. The smart turn-out and soldierly bearing of the Lancers (Military Police) in the foreground is in marked contrast to the more relaxed appearance of the *caçadores* further along.

the early 1960s was Congo (Brazzaville), and its initial guerrilla activities were limited to the adjoining Angolan enclave of Cabinda, where most of its cadres saw their first actions.

The MPLA's military wing was known as the *Exército Popular de Libertação de Angola*, or EPLA. After 1965 Zambian independence allowed it access to Eastern Angola. This was a remote and sparsely populated area, of little immediate concern to the Portuguese, and the MPLA's 'Eastern Offensive' was able to make headway. Supplies came in from Tanzania and Zambia along what the Portuguese called the 'Agostinho Neto Trail', and the MPLA was able to set up bases which they called 'Hanoi II' and 'Ho Chi Minh'. However, its units remained small, and up to 1970 at least, were equipped with a miscellany of weapons many of which dated from the Second World War. Neto met Che Guevara in 1965, and subsequently the MPLA began to receive Cuban instructors and Soviet and East German help. It also received some Chinese aid after 1970.

Meanwhile, disenchantment with Roberto's inactivity had led his 'Foreign Minister' Jonas Savimbi to leave and found his own movement in 1966. This was the *União Nacional para a Independência Total de Angola* or UNITA, whose armed forces were known as the *Forças Armadas de Liberação de Angola* (FALA). They were recruited mainly from the Ovimbundu peoples in central Angola. UNITA received some Chinese support and operated from Zambia until President Kaunda expelled it in 1968 for sabotaging the Benguela railway which carried Zambia's copper exports to the coast. Thereafter it led an increasingly shadowy existence, short of arms and with no more than 500 active guerrillas.

The three competing movements expended a good deal of effort in fighting each other rather than the Portuguese. The FNLA attacked MPLA groups trying to cross into northern Angola, while the Portuguese reported that MPLA informants often told them of the whereabouts of FNLA groups. One MPLA prisoner reported that he had spent more time fighting UNITA than he had fighting the Portuguese.

During 1968 the Portuguese went over to the offensive in eastern Angola. Despite this, the MPLA continued to make progress. At the end of 1970 it began to receive heavier weapons and was able to form *esquadrões* of 100 to 150 men which included 'artillery' sections armed with 60mm and 81mm mortars and 75mm recoilless rifles, allowing it to attack Portuguese posts. The Portuguese reacted by carrying out further extensive sweeps in 1972–3, one of which overran the MPLA's 'Ho Chi Minh' camp.

These counter-attacks amounted to a major defeat for the MPLA, and in 1973 Neto had to withdraw some 800 of his guerrillas to the safety of Congo (Brazzaville). The party fell into a state of disarray. One of its best commanders, Daniel Chipenda, openly challenged Neto's leadership and subsequently took his men over to the FNLA. The Soviet Union stopped supplying arms for fear that they would be used in factional fighting, and President Nyerere of Tanzania became so disillusioned that he persuaded the Chinese to transfer their support to Roberto's FNLA instead.

In fact, the Portuguese collapse in 1974 came just in time to save both the MPLA and UNITA from disaster. It encouraged the MPLA's supporters in the cities, especially Luanda, allowing the movement to recruit openly; it also opened the ports to shipments of Soviet arms, which were resumed because the Russians had become frightened by China's support for the FNLA. The result was that by mid-1975 the MPLA had some 20,000 troops and considerable quantities of Soviet equipment. This in turn provoked the Americans and South Africans to give the FNLA and UNITA clandestine support.

Two Portuguese conscripts off duty in Moçambique during the early 1970s. This photograph shows two versions of the post-1966 walking out dress.

The Portuguese tried to persuade the warring factions to form a coalition government, and the Algarve agreement of January 1975 provided for a 'national' army made up of 24,000 Portuguese and 8,000 each from the three liberation movements. None of them made any serious attempt to implement this, however, and the final Portuguese withdrawal in November 1975 was followed almost immediately by open conflict. The MPLA won, but only with the aid of considerable numbers of Cuban combat troops, upon whose continued presence they still depend; with UNITA still in the field dominating large areas, the echoes of that conflict are still reverberating around Southern Africa.

Guiné

The most successful liberation movement was Guiné's *Partido Africano da Independência da Guiné e Cabo Verde* or PAIGC. This was mainly because that territory was relatively small and encircled by states sympathetic to the nationalist cause, so that the greater part of it formed a kind of 'frontier belt'. The Portuguese soon came to the conclusion that the war there was unwinnable, but they could not give it up because of the effect of such an action elsewhere. As Salazar's successor Dr Caetano said, 'It is better to leave Guiné with an honourable defeat rather than to negotiate with the terrorists, opening the door to other negotiations'.

Guiné was a relatively small and impoverished colony on the West African coast, with few Portuguese settlers. Nevertheless, the spread of independence to the neighbouring ex-French states of Guinée (Conakry) and Sénégal was bound to encourage the development of a liberation movement, and this duly occurred.

The PAIGC was formed clandestinely in 1956. Its leader was Amilcar Cabral, a revolutionary Marxist. It quickly became the only resistance organisation within the territory (a rival movement known as FLING launched a few raids in 1963, but little was heard of it afterwards). This did not mean, however, that it was equally representative of all the Guinéan peoples: in particular, it had little success in penetrating the important and strongly Muslim Fula. The PAIGC also claimed to represent the nearby island province of Cabo Verde, though its position there was never strong, and in practice it inspired little or no guerrilla activity.

The PAIGC decided on armed insurrection after

Two 'Ferret' armoured cars on patrol against a tropical background. Like all Portuguese military vehicles they were painted a plain olive green. Unusually, the crews are wearing French 'OTAN' pattern steel helmets.

the so-called 'Pidjiguiti Massacre' in 1959, when a dock strike was broken up by the Portuguese police with considerable loss of life. Two years were spent on preparations. Sabotage operations began in 1961, and guerrilla warfare broke out early in 1963.

FARP (*Forças Armadas Revolucionárias de Povo*), the PAIGC's military wing, was formed in 1964. It was divided along classic revolutionary lines into a national regular force (the 'People's Army'), a district guerrilla force (the 'People's Guerrillas') and a local defence force (the 'People's Militia'). These locally based militias were consolidated as the *Forças Armadas Locais* in 1970. FARP claimed to be a collection of 'armed militants' rather than '*militaires*'. It deliberately rotated its cadres between civil and military positions and avoided creating any formal system of ranks. Some of the cadres were trained in Russia, China, Cuba and Algeria, others in Sénégal, Guinée (Conakry) or Ghana. The PAIGC was generously supported by the neighbouring and newly independent republics of Guinée (Conakry) and Sénégal. Its directorate remained in Conakry, and the Guinéean army provided equipment and training camps, and even laid on artillery barrages to cover FARP incursions.

FARP had a relatively simple organisational structure, being divided into three *Frentes* or Fronts (Eastern, Northern and Southern), whose commanders were responsible to an overall *Conselho de Guerra*. The basic unit was the *bigrupo* of between 30 and 50 men, with joint military and political commanders. FARP was well equipped with Soviet pattern small arms, including PPSh SMGs, SKS carbines and the ubiquitous AK-47, though it also possessed other models such as Thompson SMGs and Breda machine guns. The provision of heavier weapons was limited by transportation difficulties and they were mainly restricted to Soviet pattern 82mm mortars, Cuban bazookas and Chinese recoilless rifles. These transportation problems led the FARP to form its own 'navy' of light vessels based in the Republic of Guinée.

By 1968 the PAIGC claimed to control some two-thirds of the territory and 50 per cent of the population. It had set up a system of regional and

A pause on the road. Note the mixture of 1961 and 1963 pattern field caps, the canvas boots and the Portuguese flag on the jeep. The white lettering on the bonnet reads '*Exército*' (Army).

25-pdr. guns of an African artillery unit lined up during the early 1960s. The guns were painted olive green, while the gunners wore olive steel helmets and light khaki shirts, shorts and gaiters.

local administration within its 'liberated areas' and founded schools and hospitals. The Portuguese had been forced back into the main towns and some coastal areas and their morale was low. However, the arrival of Brig. Spínola brought about a change of fortune. He initiated a civic action programme, promoted black Guinéans, and created an alternative representative system culminating in a People's Congress. His inspiring leadership did much to help the Portuguese to regain both territory and influence.

These reverses led to a reorganisation of FARP, whose regular strength was approximately 5,000. In 1972 the 'Fronts' were broken up to form about a dozen 'Army Corps' under the direct control by the *Conselho de Guerra*. These consisted of up to five *bigrupos*, one of which was an 'artillery' unit, plus smaller specialised units, and had a total strength of 400–450 men. Most were to be based outside Guiné, occasionally sending 'incursion groups' of up to 120 men to attack specific objectives. FARP's presence inside the country was restricted to a number of small, highly mobile Commando units, each approximately 48 strong. Both these developments clearly reflected Portuguese successes after 1968.

However, this enforced reorganisation was also accompanied by an increased flow of sophisticated weaponry. In 1971 FARP began to receive Soviet 122mm rockets, which they nicknamed 'Grads'. FARP's incursion groups now included artillery units, and there were even some small armoured units equipped with PT-76s, though these do not appear to have seen action. Moreover, FARP was able to challenge the Portuguese command of the air. It began to receive Soviet SAM missiles in 1973, and even support from a few MiG sorties launched from the safety of Guinée (Conakry); and a number of Portuguese planes were shot down. These factors, together with a decline in Portuguese morale after Spínola's departure in 1972, enabled FARP to attack and capture Guiledje, an important Portuguese military base commanding supply routes from Guinée (Conakry).

Cabral was assassinated in Conakry in 1973 by a disgruntled former member of the PAIGC's Supreme Council (Portuguese complicity was alleged but denied). The PAIGC went ahead with elections for a National Assembly, and proclaimed the independence of the new Republic of Guiné-Bissau in September 1973, nearly a year before it was formally granted by Portugal.

Moçambique
Nationalist activity began relatively late in Moçambique. Three separate movements with strong regional bases were formed during 1960–61, and these joined together in 1962 as the *Frente Libertação de Moçambique* or FRELIMO. Julius Nyerere, president of newly independent Tanganyika (later Tanzania), was sympathetic, and offered sanctuary to the nationalists. The new movement elected as its leader a man who was not associated with any of its constituent parties; Eduardo Mondlane, a southerner who had been educated in South Africa and the United States as well as Portugal, and who had been both a university lecturer and a UN researcher.

FRELIMO remained a somewhat fragile co-

A patrol in the bush. This photograph gives a good idea of the conditions throughout much of Angola and Moçambique. The vehicle is a UNIMOG 4x4, and the men carry standard G-3 rifles.

alition. Its members differed both ethnically and ideologically, and Mondlane had great difficulty in holding it together. Many of the original founders left to form splinter movements of their own, and at least one of these (the Chinese-supported COREMO), was able to put its own guerrillas into the field. There were disputes about strategy within FRELIMO itself. To begin with, some activists wanted to launch a lightning attack on the capital, despite the fact that the Portuguese had been steadily reinforcing their garrisons after the revolt in Angola. Others wanted to incite the peasants against the Portuguese settlers. A third group, which included Samora Machel, argued for a protracted guerrilla struggle along classic Communist lines; and it was these who finally carried the day, though only after fierce argument.

FRELIMO did not begin its operations until 1964, though it had been sending groups to Algeria for training since 1962. The initial plan was to organise risings over the country as a whole, but the South African, Malawian and Rhodesian authorities closed their borders to the nationalists, so that the southern and central fronts soon collapsed.

The only remaining route was across the frontier from Tanzania, and penetration was restricted to the remote northern provinces of Cabo Delgado and Niassa. Here the Portuguese were initially relatively weak, and FRELIMO found it possible to establish a number of 'liberated areas' (though this only meant places where they exercised influence rather than genuinely independent enclaves).

FRELIMO's military wing was known as the FPLM. According to Mondlane, it began with only some 250 trained men. These operated in units of 12 to 15 men from the sanctuary of Tanzanian territory, and were poorly equipped with bolt-action Mauser rifles, MAT-49 sub-machine guns, grenades and mines. By 1965, however, they were operating in company-strength units, and by 1966 in battalions. FPLM used 'positional' titles rather than formal ranks. A central command was established in 1966 to co-ordinate activities within the different regions. By 1967 FRELIMO claimed to have 8,000 men, excluding the People's Militias in the northern 'liberated zones'. The movement continued to enjoy Tanzanian support, and its main training camp was located at Kongwa in southern Tanzania.

Until 1970 arms came mainly from the Soviet Union. However, Chinese instructors had arrived in Tanzania, and Chinese versions of standard Warsaw Pact weapons began to reach the insurgents, who reportedly preferred them. Heavy weapons were limited to 75mm recoilless rifles, 82mm and 129mm mortars, Chinese-made Type 56 (RPF-2), Type 69 (RPF-7) and Soviet 122mm rockets; the guerrillas' most effective weapon remained the mine.

Initially, FRELIMO was divided into a military wing (the FPLM under the Department of Defence), and a civil wing (the Department of the Interior) which took responsibility for the administration of the liberated areas together with all political matters. This division led to conflicts which reflected more fundamental disagreements over policy. Mondlane and Machel wanted a movement committed to revolutionary socialism, but there was strong opposition from a more conservative faction based on the important Makonde people of northern Moçambique, who provided much of FRELIMO's manpower. Their leaders wanted the restoration of traditional authority and advocated control by a Council of Chiefs instead of the Central Committee. Matters came to a head at FRELIMO's Second Congress of 1968. The traditionalists lost the struggle, partly because Nyerere refused to back their demand for a separatist Biafra-like Makonde state. Deserted by the Tanzanians and expelled by FRELIMO, the conservatives found themselves isolated, and some three months later their leader Kavandame went over to the Portuguese. Shortly afterwards Mondlane was killed by a parcel bomb and was succeeded by Machel.

The new leadership quickly abolished the old division between civil and military. The functions of the Department of the Interior were taken over by FRELIMO's Political Commissars, who ranked equally with the military Operational Chiefs within the Provincial Commands. The military sections were divided into Sabotage, Materials, Reconnaissance, Infantry and Artillery. Each sector had its guerrilla 'battalion', which was split up into three or four 150-man companies, each with its own base. These companies formed the field units. They were further sub-divided into platoons (36 men), sections (12) and finally, groups (three men). The 'regulars' were backed up by local People's Militias within the liberated areas (though during the 1967–68 crisis the Makonde militiamen in Cabo Delgado actually turned against the FPLM and killed at least one of its senior commanders).

After 1970 the FPLM managed to break out of the northern provinces. Using Zambia as a base it succeeded in opening a new front in Tete, where the Portuguese were constructing a huge man-made lake behind the Cabora Bassa dam, partly to form a barrier against any such penetration. The Portuguese responded with a major operation ('Gordian Knot') in the north; but the FPLM continued to extend its influence, spreading southwards along the line of the Zambezi River to threaten what FRELIMO called the Portuguese 'spinal column'. By late 1973 its advanced guerrilla groups were operating not far from Beira. By this stage the more regular FPLM units in the north had started to receive SAM-7 anti-aircraft missiles and were able to attack fortified posts with reasonable prospects of success.

Portuguese resistance slackened after the coup of

Mine clearance. The lightness and informality of Portuguese field dress is obvious, and its marked contrast to the flak vests and steel helmets worn by US troops in Vietnam reflects the relatively smaller scale and lighter weapons which characterised most fighting.

April 1974, and the FPLM's southern offensive gathered pace rapidly. Unofficial local ceasefires came into force, and these were followed by a formal agreement in September. This prompted a brief rising by diehard white settlers, but the new Portuguese government refused it support and it collapsed after three days. Last-minute attempts to form more moderate African political parties also failed, and FRELIMO ended up as undisputed masters of the new state of Moçambique.

The Portuguese Forces

The Portuguese armed forces have a long and proud history, which is relatively little known outside Portugal itself. They drove out the Moors during the Middle Ages, defeated the Spaniards to restore their country's independence during the 17th century, and fought valiantly and effectively with Wellington during the Peninsular War. They also mounted innumerable colonial campaigns in Africa, Asia and the Americas. Although they had not seen any major action since the First World War, when a Portuguese Expeditionary Force had fought with the Allies on the Western Front, Portugal became a founder member of NATO, and this gave her access to modern Western military doctrines and equipment.

The armed forces were closely identified with Dr Salazar's 'New State', and the president was invariably a general or an admiral. The officer corps itself was drawn from the traditional élite, and senior officers commonly held concurrent appointments as directors of major commercial organisations. The rank and file, on the other hand, were conscripts from Portugal's predominantly rural population: tough, uncomplaining and industrious. The normal term of service was two years, with up to four years in specialist arms and the Navy and Air Force.

In 1960 the metropolitan army had 16 infantry regiments (of three battalions each), ten *Caçadores* ('Hunters', or Rifles) battalions, three machine gun battalions, one tank, eight cavalry, two engineer and 11 artillery regiments (five light, one mountain, two AA, two coastal and one independent), plus one each railway, telegraphist and bridging battalions. Other units were raised in the Açores (two independent battalions) and Madeira (one battalion). There were three 'triangular' divisions, of which the 3rd was assigned to NATO. Metropolitan regiments bore numbers, but had traditional regional associations (the 1st, for instance, was linked with Queluz near Lisbon), and long histories. As in other armies, the cavalry proper had been converted to armour, but the Lancers had been turned into military police in 1953. Artillery and other specialist arms followed conventional practice; but the Portuguese Army was unusual in maintaining a separate Staff corps, recruited from among the captains by competitive examination. It was also unusual in that there was only one general rank (four, five and six star 'ranks' were technically appointments), a provision which tended to encourage factionalism.

There were certain other military and paramilitary forces. The Air Force maintained a battalion of *pára-quedistas* first raised in 1955–56; while the Navy had its *fuzileiros*, equivalent to the French Navy's *fusiliers marins* (this branch was inactive during the 1950s but was recreated in February 1961). There was a 10,000-strong Republican Guard. In addition, there were the Portuguese Legion and the *Brigada Naval*, both voluntary and notably right wing political militias. Founded in 1936, the Legion had once sent volunteers to fight for the Nationalists in the Spanish Civil War, but by 1960 its members were fairly elderly and it was really no more than a kind of Home Guard.

This display, photographed on a barracks wall in Moçambique, shows the G-3 rifle and other individual Portuguese infantry equipment. The legend means 'Look after these for your life'.

The Army's units were organised along conventional lines. An infantry division had three infantry regiments; three 105mm artillery groups (54 guns in all); one 140mm group (18 guns); an AA group with 32 40mm Bofors guns; an anti-tank group of three squadrons with 20 guns each; a reconnaissance squadron; engineer, signals and medical battalions; and supply, ordnance and reinforcement companies, plus a band.

The infantry regiment consisted of three infantry battalions, a heavy mortar company (three mortar platoons and a range- and direction-finding platoon), and a service company (transport, ordnance, maintenance and medical platoons). An anti-tank company was planned but had not yet been included. The infantry battalions consisted of three rifle companies (each with three rifle platoons of three sections each), a support platoon (with separate mortar, light machine gun and recoilless rifle sections), and an HQ company (with signals, engineer and medical platoons).

The artillery *grupo* consisted of three *batarias* of six guns each. The reconnaissance squadrons were subdivided into three platoons (troops), each with two armoured cars, one APC, one car and seven jeeps, plus an HQ platoon with one armoured car, two APCs and another 16 jeeps and trucks, with a strength of 181 men and an armament which included nine 60mm and three 81mm mortars. There were also independent reconnaissance platoons, each of three sections with two cars and two jeeps each, plus an HQ section with another car and jeep. These platoons had a strength of 41 officers and men with seven 60mm mortars.

Equipment

The Army had a varied collection of small arms. The main pistol was the m/943 9mm Parabellum (in fact the well known Luger: the designation m/943 signified that it had been officially adopted in 1943). This was about to be replaced by the m/961 Walther. The basic rifle was the m/937 7.9mm Mauser, which had replaced the older 65mm Mauser-Vergeiro and which was identical with the German Kar 98k. This was about to be replaced by the m/961 7.62mm G-3, a licence-built copy of the well known West German weapon, though considerable quantities of the m/962 7.62mm FN/FAL were also obtained later. Each rifle section had four riflemen equipped to fire m/953 Energa rifle grenades. The sub-machine gun stock included the m/942 Steyr and the m/948 FBP, the only Portuguese-designed weapon in use. Later, supplies of Belgian Vigneron and West German-made UZI SMGs were also obtained: both were

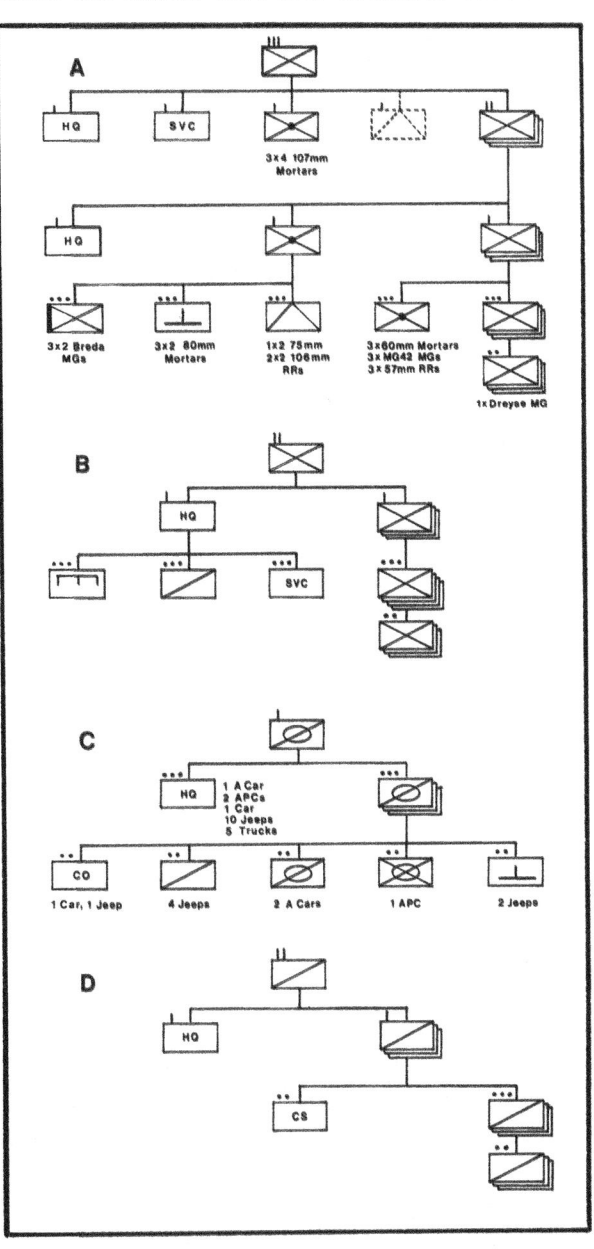

Portuguese unit organisations. (A) *Regimento de Infantaria* 1963 (no units of this size actually saw operational service in Africa, but the chart shows the standard battalion structure and the diversity of weapons in use at the time). (B) *Batalhão de Caçadores Especiais* mid-1960s onwards (showing how the Heavy Weapons Company was converted into a fourth 'combat group'). (C) *Esquadrão de Reconhecimento* 1963–74 ('Jeep' indicates any small 4 × 4 vehicle, frequently a Unimog). (D) *Grupo de Cavalaria* c.1970.

given the designation m/961. All these were in the standard 9mm calibre. The infantry section's light machine gun was the elderly m/938 7.92mm Dreyse (a predecessor of the German MG34): the support platoon's MG section had the m/944 7.92mm (the German MG42), and the battalion's heavy weapons company had the equally elderly m/938 7.92mm Breda. All these were subsequently phased out in favour of the m/962 7.92mm (a licence-built copy of the Bundeswehr's MG42-59). The heavy machine gun (held at regimental level and assigned mainly to AA defence) was the sturdy m/951 12.7mm (0.5in.) Browning. The support platoon's mortar section was equipped with the US M2 60mm (designated m/952), the heavy weapons company with the venerable French Brandt 81mm (designated m/937 8cm) and the regimental heavy mortar company with the US M2 107mm (designated m/951) or an equivalent. There were also m/955 60mm and m/952 89mm *Lança Granadas Fogute* (bazookas).

The heavier weapons were equally variegated.

The standard field gun was the US M101A1 105mm, but there were considerable numbers of old 75mm and ex-British 25-pdr. and 5.5 in. guns in use as well. The armoured units were equipped with US M-24, M-47 and M-48 tanks, and the reconnaissance units with a mixture of Daimler scout cars and Panhard AML-90, EBR-75, 'Fox', Humber Mk IV or locally made 'Chaimite' armoured cars (the latter a version of the US 'Commando'), while their supporting infantry sections were carried in either EBR-VTT APCs or the older US M-3 half-tracks. The newer EBR-75 armoured cars were generally combined with the EBR-VTTs and the older 'Fox' cars with the M-3 half tracks. The independent reconnaissance platoons used the lighter Panhard AML or Daimler scout cars (the latter with a slightly top-heavy octagonal turret added).

Initially, most of the vehicles were American in origin. The most common was the well known jeep, supplemented by the equally familiar Dodge 3/4 ton 4 × 4 and 2.5 ton GMC 6 × 6 trucks. An infantry regiment had 209 Jeeps, 42 Dodges and 79 GMCs, together with 18 BMW motorcycles. During the mid-1960s many of these vehicles were

Dragoons in Angola, early 1970s. The black trooper holding the horse's head is wearing the standard web waist belt and pouches.

A selection of unit shields. These semi-official distinctions were worn on either chest or upper left sleeve. *Top left* is 1578 Recce Sqn., a green vehicle on a yellow/red shield; *top centre*, 2022 Recce Sqn., a black fox's head and white swords on a yellow/red shield; *top right* BCAÇ 2889, blue and red quarters with a yellow saltire and white devices; *bottom left* BCAÇ 2888, also quartered blue and red with yellow saltire and white symbols; *bottom centre* CCAÇ 2727, a black map of Moçambique on red, the Portuguese arms on green and black eagle and rifles on silver; *bottom right* BCAV 705, dark grey on silver blue.

replaced by Austin 'Gypsies', Landrovers, Berliet lorries and licence-built 'UNIMOG' 4 × 4 utility trucks, which became the workhorses of the Portuguese army.

Organisation of Overseas Forces

The organisation and equipment of the overseas forces followed similar lines to those of the metropolitan troops, as indeed they had done for most of the imperial period. The main exception had been the years from 1900 to 1951, when there was a separate colonial army based on native *companhias indígenas* stiffened with a small number of Europeans. These forces had been relatively small: during the later 1940s, for instance, the Guiné garrison consisted of one *Caçadores* company, one engineer company, a small artillery battery and a band, all natives. The constitutional change from 'Colony' to 'Overseas Province' meant that this system was no longer appropriate, however; in 1951 the Army took over responsibility for the colonial units and the term *caçador indígena* disappeared.

In theory, male Portuguese citizens living in the overseas provinces were supposed to do their military service in their local units just as they did in the home country. This applied to the *assimilados* as well as the whites. In practice, however, few *assimilados* were actually called up, and the proportion of African NCOs actually fell because few of the recruits were able to meet the educational qualifications. Most posts above corporal were filled by whites, the officers and senior NCOs by regulars from the metropolitan army and other NCOs by locally recruited conscript *milicianos*. The rank and file remained a mixture of *indígena* volunteers and conscripts of all races. Relations remained good; the Belgians in the Congo, who naturally took a keen interest in their neighbours' affairs, commented on the rapport which existed between white and black Portuguese soldiers as compared with the relationship within their own *Force Publique*.

The Army re-introduced a conventional regimental structure. Angola and Moçambique were each to have three infantry regiments, one group of motorised cavalry, four artillery groups and a battalion of engineers. Guiné was to have one infantry battalion and an artillery battery, Cabo Verde two infantry companies and an artillery battery, and São Tomé e Principe one infantry company. It was also planned to revive the old militia force, which had been allowed to lapse during the 20th century, though this was not taken in hand before 1961.

In 1960 the Army as a whole was reorganised into five *Regiões*. Portugal itself was divided into the Lisbon, 1st (Northern) and 2nd (Southern) Regions. Angola and São Tomé e Principe became the 3rd Region (sub-divided into Northern, Central, Southern, Eastern, Cabinda and São Tomé Commands); and Moçambique the 4th (sub-divided into Northern, Central and Southern Commands). The Açores, Madeira, Cabo Verde, Goa, Macau and Timor became independent Territorial Commands. In 1962 this organisation was slightly modified, Angola and Moçambique becoming 'named' rather than numbered regions, though with no alterations to the sub-divisions. The Air Force had its own organisation, with metropolitan Portugal, the Açores, Madeira, Cabo Verde and Guiné constituting the 1st Region, Angola and São Tomé e Principe the 2nd, and Moçambique and the Far Eastern provinces the 3rd.

The Portuguese were not taken completely by surprise by the outbreak of guerrilla warfare in Angola in 1961, though they certainly underestimated its seriousness. They had already begun building up their forces: the Portuguese contingent was expanded from 1,000 in 1958 to 3,000 by 1960. The Air Force began establishing bases there in the late 1950s, created a new *pára-quedista* battalion (the

Air Force *pára-quedistas* on parade. They wear emerald green berets with the post-1966 badge (a silver eagle in a gilt wreath) and carry FPB sub-machine guns. The four figures in the foreground each wear a different company-colour scarf: from left to right crimson, yellow, green and white.

21st) for service in Angola, and staged demonstrations of paratroop dropping and napalm bombing (Operation 'Himba', April 1959).

The paratroops were soon in action, first against the unorganised rebels of 'Maria's War', then against the far more serious UPA-organised revolt in the north. The Portuguese elements of the provincial forces were also used, along with a battalion of *fuzileiros* and some 2,000 armed settlers, who were formed into a *Corpo de Voluntários*, some of whom were certainly responsible for counter-atrocities. There seems to have been some reluctance to use the province's black troops, however, and metropolitan reinforcements were called for.

This was a time-honoured practice. The metropolitan army was accustomed to despatching substantial expeditionary forces to Africa (it had sent far more European troops there during the First World War than had either Britain or France), and it was familiar with the problems. Two battalions were sent in May 1960 (these seem to have been Nos. 89 and 92), and these were followed by a series of others as the system swung into action. At the same time, the Air Force began organising additional *caçadores pára-quedista* battalions in the other African provinces (BCP 12 in Guiné and BCP 31 and 32 in Moçambique).

The mobilisation system itself was something of a departure from previous practice. During the First World War the units sent to Africa had been the 3rd Battalions of existing metropolitan regiments. The 1960 system involved the creation of independent, separately numbered light infantry battalions, which were designated *Caçadores Especiais* (the Navy formed equivalent *Fuzileiros Especiais*). These were organised along standard infantry battalion lines but with certain changes designed to fit them for an independent counter-insurgency role. Initially these were restricted to giving the HQ company a *conselho administrativo* or enlarged staff with an expanded intelligence section. Later, however, the support platoon was abolished and the rifle companies were sub-divided into four 'combat groups' each instead of three rifle platoons. New specialisations such as *pisteiros* (trackers) and mine detectors were introduced. These light infantry battalions were temporary units which were disbanded when their members' terms of service

21st Bn. Pára-quedistas' chaplain offers some reassurance before a jump. The officer behind him wears the pre-1966 beret badge, crossed rifles superimposed on a parachute. Note the jump boots and US pattern steel helmets.

had ended. Most were raised by the existing metropolitan infantry regiments; but because they were all designated *caçadores* before leaving for Africa no metropolitan infantry served there as such (as far as the ordinary soldier was concerned, this distinction amounted to little more than a change of badge on leaving Portugal). Some, however, were provided by other arms after a two-month conversion course—such as BART (Artillery Battalion) 635, whose parent unit was the 1st Artillery Regiment and which served as infantry in Angola from 1964 to 1966. The cavalry regiments generally formed independent reconnaissance squadrons or platoons for service in Africa. These were organised on the same basis as the metropolitan units. No tank units were sent to Africa.

The numbering system used remains confusing to the outsider. In principle, each company was given its own serial number and the battalion another. This latter was sometimes part of the same series (thus, BART 635 consisted of CARTs nos. 632, 633 and 634), but this relationship tended to break down in the infantry and cavalry with the proliferation of independent companies, such as CCAÇ 2727 (an independent company raised by the Açores-based Infantry Battalion no. 18). BCAÇ 2927, for instance, was composed of CCAÇ nos. 2780, 2781 and 2782. Since the numbers were issued

21

serially, they got higher and higher with the passage of time. Numbers in the range 1–1,000 served during 1961–67, the '1,000' series indicated service between 1967 and 1969, the '2,000' series 1969–71, the '3,000' series 1971–72 and the '4,000' series 1973–75. For some unknown reason there were also a few numbers in the '7,000' and '8,000' series. Unfortunately, there would not be space to set out a complete Order of Battle of the metropolitan units even if it were possible to compile one at present.

These metropolitan units should not be confused with the provincially based ones. These remained in existence in order to train locally recruited conscripts, and their infantry regiments began to maintain their own field units in the same way as the metropolitan ones. Originally temporary formations, these field units came to be regarded as permanent ones. Initially the expansion process was somewhat haphazard, but the matter was taken in hand by *Ordem do Exército* (Army Order) No. 2 of February 1967, which rationalised the numbering system for all the overseas provinces.

Pre-1967 Title and Location	Post-1967 Title
Cabo Verde	
1a Companhia de Caçadores (Praia)	Companhia de Caçadores no. 1
2a Companhia de Caçadores (Mindelo)	Companhia de Caçadores no. 2
Bataria de Artilharia de Guarnição (Mindelo)	Bataria de Artilharia de Guarnição no. 3*
Guiné	
1a Companhia de Caçadores (Farim)	Companhia de Caçadores no. 3
2a Companhia de Caçadores (Buba)	Companhia de Caçadores no. 4*
3a Companhia de Caçadores (Nova Lamego)	Companhia de Caçadores no. 5
4a Companhia de Caçadores (Bedanda)	Companhia de Caçadores no. 6
Bataria de Artilharia de Campanha (Bissau)	Bataria de Artilharia de Campanha no. 1
Sao Tomé	
Companhia de Caçadores de S. Tomé (S. Tomé)	Companhia de Caçadores no. 7
Angola	
Regimento de Infantaria de Luanda (Luanda)	Regimento de Infantaria no. 20
Regimento de Infantaria de Nova Lisboa (Nova Lisboa)	Regimento de Infantaria no. 21
Regimento de Infantaria de Sá da Bandeira (Sá da Bandeira)	Regimento de Infantaria no. 22
Batalhão de Caçadores no. 248 (Cabinda)	Batalhão de Caçadores no. 11
Batalhão de Caçadores no. 3 (Carmona)	Batalhão de Caçadores no. 12
Batalhão de Caçadores no. 443 (Salazar)	Batalhão de Caçadores no. 13
Grupo de Artilharia de Campanha de Luanda (Luanda)	Grupo de Artilharia de Campanha no. 1
Grupo de Artilharia de Campanha de Nova Lisboa (N. Lisboa)	Grupo de Artilharia de Campanha no. 2
Grupo de Artilharia de Campanha de Sá da Bandera (S. da B.)	Grupo de Artilharia de Campanha no. 3*
Grupo de Artilharia Antiaérea de Angola (Benguela)	Grupo de Artilharia Antiaérea no. 4*
Bataria de Artilharia de Defesa da Costa (Luanda)	Bataria de Artilharia de Defesa da Costa no. 2*
Bataria de Artilharia de Defesa da Costa (Lobito)	Bataria de Artilharia de Defesa da Costa no. 3*
Grupo de Reconhecimento de Angola (Silva Porto)	Grupo de Cavalaria no. 1
Batalhão de Engenharia (Luanda)	Batalhão de Engenharia no. 1
Batalhão de Transmissões (Luanda)	Batalhão de Transmissões no. 1
Moçambique	
Regimento de Infantaria de Lorenço Marques (L. Marques)	Regimento de Infantaria no. 23*
Regimento de Infantaria de Beira (Vila Pery)	Regimento de Infantaria no. 24*
Regimento de Infantaria de Nampula (Nampula)	Regimento de Infantaria no. 25*
Batalhão de Caçadores de Porto Amelia (Porto Amelia)	Batalhão de Caçadores no. 14
Batalhão de Caçadores de Nampula (Nampula)	Batalhão de Caçadores no. 15
Batalhão de Caçadores de Beira (Beira)	Batalhão de Caçadores no. 16
Batalhão de Caçadores de Boane (Maxixe)	Batalhão de Caçadores no. 17
Batalhão de Caçadores de Lorenço Marques (L. Marques)	Batalhão de Caçadores no. 18
Batalhão de Caçadores no. 6 (Nova Freixo)	Batalhão de Caçadores no. 19
Batalhão de Caçadores no. 7 (Vila Pery)	Batalhão de Caçadores no. 20

The Portuguese Forces in Action

The Portuguese introduced sweeping political changes designed to redress African grievances. The distinction between *indígena* and *assimilado* was abolished and all Africans became Portuguese citizens. This freed the *indígenas* from their forced labour obligations, but it also exposed them to the Portuguese conscription laws. In practice, these were not rigorously enforced and a 1967 estimate of the 'provincial' forces in Angola indicated a 3:1 ratio of whites to blacks (though it was no more than 1:6 in Guiné, where there were hardly any white settlers). These 'provincial' units were the only ones to be multi-racial, and it is they which account for the great majority of the photographs published during the period which show whites and blacks serving side by side in the same unit.

The war itself remained small scale. The Portuguese lost or abandoned a few posts in northern Angola during the 1961 revolt, but these had all been re-occupied by the end of the year. Elsewhere the guerrillas lacked the firepower to attack Portuguese fortified posts successfully until the very end of the war. For the Portuguese it was a matter of keeping these supplied, trying to locate and destroy the small guerrilla bands, and attempting to counteract their influence with the local populations.

It was a war of ambushes, with the mine probably causing about 70 per cent of Portuguese casualties overall. Practically all the roads in Portuguese Africa had dirt surfaces, which made mines relatively easy to conceal. The answer lay in tarring the roads, and the Portuguese engineers performed prodigies of labour in this respect. In the interim, convoys had to be preceded by *pesquizadors*, (sappers with mine detectors) or by men armed with long pointed sticks (*picas*) with which they prodded every suspect patch.

The garrisons of the major fortified posts were normally provided by the conscript or *milicias* infantry units, and most *caçadores* battalions had their companies split up and allocated in this way. Convoy escort duties were undertaken by the reconnaissance units, in conjunction with combat groups from the garrison units. The task of carrying the war to the guerrillas was entrusted to the *unidades de intervenção*, highly mobile élite units who could be rushed to an area as soon as a guerrilla band was contacted, or else carry out long-range

Pre-1967 Title and Location	Post-1967 Title
Grupo de Artilharia de Campanha de Lorenço Marques (Boane)	Grupo de Artilharia de Campanha no. 4*
Grupo de Artilharia de Campanha de Beira (Vila Pery)	Grupo de Artilharia de Campanha no. 5*
Grupo de Artilharia de Campanha de Nampula (Nampula)	Grupo de Artilharia de Campanha no. 6
Grupo de Artilharia Antiaérea de Moçambique (Beira)	Grupo de Artilharia Antiaérea no. 5*
Grupo de Artilharia de Guarnição de Lorenço Marques (L. Marques)	Grupo de Artilharia de Guarnição no. 1*
Bataria Independente de Artilharia de Defesa da Costa de Beira (Beira)	Bataria de Artilharia de Defesa da Costa no. 4*
Bataria de Artilharia de Costa de Lorenço Marques (Boane)	Bataria de Artilharia de Defesa da Costa no. 5
Grupo de Reconhecimento de Moçambique (Lorenço Marques)	Grupo de Cavalaria no. 2*
Esquadrão de Reconhecimento de Lorenço Marques (L. Marques)	Esquadrão de Cavalaria no. 1
Esquadrão de Reconhecimento de Vila Pery (Vila Pery)	Esquadrão de Cavalaria no. 2
Esquadrão de Reconhecimento de Nampula (Nampula)	Esquadrão de Cavalaria no. 3
Batalhão de Engenharia (Nampula)	Batalhão de Engenharia no. 2
Companhia de Transmissões (L. Marques)	Companhia de Transmissões no. 1

* = unit authorised but currently inactive

(For the sake of completeness, it might be added that Macau was allocated Companhias de Caçadores nos. 8–9, Bataria de Artilharia de Campanha no. 2 and Esquadrão de Cavalaria no. 4, while Timor was allocated Companhias de Caçadores nos. 10–14, Bataria de Artilharia de Campanha no. 3 and Esquadrão de Cavalaria no. 5)

sweeps in the virgin bush. This was a very French concept (the French were the acknowledged experts in counter-insurgency warfare after their years of experience in Indo-China and Algeria), and the élite intervention units echoed French practice, consisting as they did of the *pára-quedistas*, *fuzileiros* and *commandos*.

The latter were a wartime innovation. A Commando Training School was set up at Lamego in Portugal in 1962, and subsequently similar schools were established in Angola (Luanda), Guiné and Moçambique (Montepuez). They began to produce small assault infantry companies (100–150 men) recruited from volunteers. Some of these *commandos* were composed of metropolitan Portuguese and were mainly white, others were recruited from the provincial units and were multi-racial or, in the case of Guiné's élite Commando Battalion, almost entirely black. Selection criteria were high, and only some 25 per cent of the volunteers succeeding in qualifying for the coveted unit shield. The troops reportedly elected their NCOs, who in turn elected the officers.

If these units were French-inspired, the *dragões* (dragoons) were a wholly Portuguese innovation. Horsed cavalry had long been used in both southern Angola and Moçambique, which were tsetse-free, and the Portuguese simply resurrected the idea. Cavalry could cover up to 50km a day, were less vulnerable to mines and ambushes than vehicles and were better able to detect guerrillas in bush country than helicopter-borne troops. Moreover, the cost of one 'Berliet' truck would purchase enough horses to mount a platoon. The first mounted platoon was constituted around Silva Porto in Eastern Angola in 1966; it soon proved its effectiveness and in 1968 it became the three-squadron *Grupo de Cavalaria No. 1*. The term *dragões*, which was unofficial but widely used, indicated that the troopers operated as mounted infantry. Each squadron had three platoons (each of three sections divided into two *esquadras* of two *trios* each); a support section (one MG and three rifle grenadiers); an orderly, a bugler and a farrier (the mounts did not have horseshoes). Each dragoon carried a Walther pistol in addition to his G-3 rifle. In 1971 the same principle was extended to Moçambique.

The Air Force played an important rôle in supporting the ground forces. By the late 1960s it had about 21,000 men in Africa, with some 150 combat aircraft ranging from venerable but effective T-6s, B-26s and PV-2s to more modern F-84, F-86 and Fiat G91s. There were some 66 Noratlas, C-45, C-47, DC-6 and Boeing 707 transport planes; a number of light army co-operation aircraft such as 'Austers' and Do. 27s; and 85 Alouette III and SA-330 Puma helicopters. The Air Force bases (No. 1 in Cabo Verde, No. 12 in Guiné, Nos. 2, 3, 4 and 9 in Angola and Nos. 5, 6, 7, 8 and 10 in Moçambique) were guarded by *Polícia Aérea* (Air Force Police) organised and equipped like *caçadores*.

The Navy also played an important rôle. Apart from its *fuzileiros*, it also provided ships to patrol the coastal waters and launch seaborne landings. Seven frigates (four of the French '*Commandant Rivière*' class

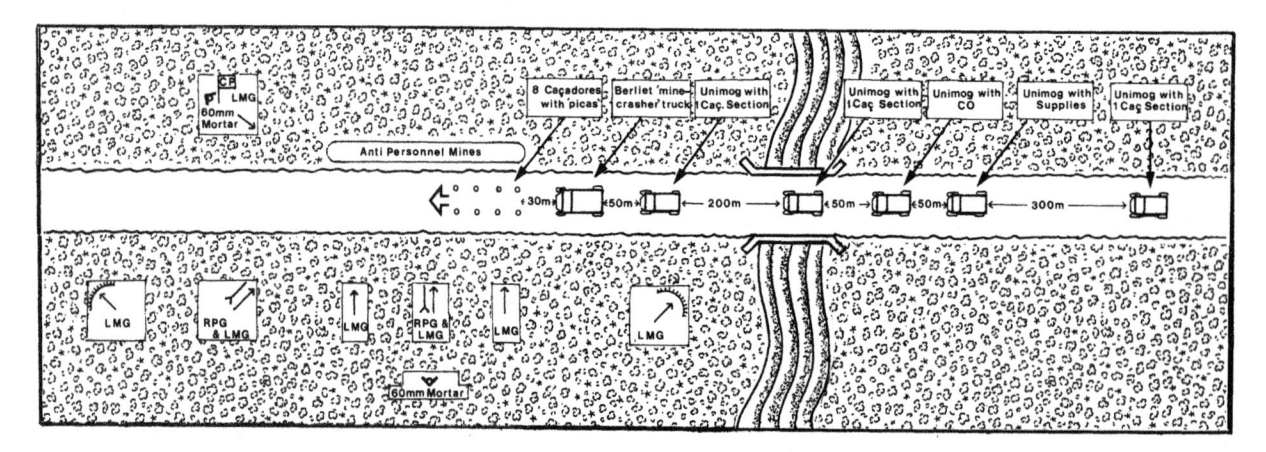

A guerrilla ambush on a Portuguese column. The Portuguese unit is a *caçadores* Combat Group, and the vehicle distributions and spacings are based on official Portuguese regulations. The ambush is based on one carried out by the MPLA in Eastern Angola in 1973 and described by Basil Davidson in his *The People's Cause* (Longman 1981).

1: General, Tropical Dress Uniform, 1961
2: Tenente Coronel, Air Force, Tropical Uniform, 1961
3: Segundo Cabo, Infantry, 1960

A

1: General, Overseas Service Dress, 1961
2: Soldado, Infantry, Field Dress, 1961
3: Cabo, Caçadores, Combat Dress, 1961

1: Nurse, Combat Dress, 1961
2: Capitão, Cavalry, Walking-Out Dress, 1961
3: Soldado, Signals, Working Dress, 1963

1: Subtenente, Fuzileiros, Combat Dress, 1964
2: Primeiro Cabo, Engineers, Working Dress, 1966
3: Segundo Sargento, Artillery, Service Dress, 1966

D

1: Capitão, Commandos, Parade Dress, 1970
2: Soldado, Dragoons, Field Dress, 1972
3: Warrant Officer, Paratroops, Combat Dress, 1974

1: Volunteer, OPVDCA, 1970
2: Volunteer, Grupos Especiais, 1972
3: Primeiro Sargento, Police/Milicia, 1973

1: Angolan FNLA 'regular', 1964
2: Angolan MPLA guerrilla, 1970
3: Angolan UNITA guerrilla, 1974

1: Guinéan PAIGC 'regular', 1974
2: Moçambiquan FRELIMO guerrilla, 1970
3: Moçambiquan 'regular', 1974

Caçadores descend from an 'Alouette' helicopter. The Portuguese Air Force's red on white 'Cross of Christ' is painted on its underside.

and three of the American '*Dealey*' class) were modified to carry *fuzileiro* landing parties. Three ex-British LCTs and 12 smaller landing craft were also used, along with six corvettes of the '*João Countinho*' class and ten '*Cacine*' patrol boats.

The war also involved controlling the civil population. Here the Portuguese borrowed the British idea of the fortified hamlet, which they called an *aldeamento*. These were set up in every area infiltrated by the guerrillas, and the population was concentrated within them both to isolate, and to protect them from the guerrillas. At the same time the authorities attempted to initiate 'hearts and minds' campaigns, setting up schools and medical posts staffed by young *milicianos* from the neighbouring military posts.

The defence of outlying settlements, coupled with the new *aldeamento* programme, required a massive expansion of the auxiliary forces, which came under the civilian administration. This controlled the *Polícia de Segurança Pública* (PSP) and its African constables, who were known as *cipaios*. It was also responsible for the various white volunteer groups (these included the Volunteer Corps set up in response to the Angolan emergency, a Rural Guard composed of older and less mobile farmers, and certain specialised units such as Air and Railway Brigades). In 1962 these were integrated into a new *Organisação Provincial de Voluntários e Defesa Civil de Angola* (OPVDCA). A similar organisation was set up in Moçambique (OPVDCM). Their members undertook guard duties and were also involved in escorting convoys. The Portuguese also mobilised the native population, many of whom were opposed to the guerrillas on ethnic or even religious grounds. A *Corpo Militar de Segunda Linha* or *Milícia* was established. This was a local corps, organised in platoons with a police sergeant (usually white) supported by a corporal in command. They were to be found in the cities and small towns, but their main rôle was as a kind of Home Guard for the defence of the *aldeamentos*.

The civil administration was also responsible for the much-feared PIDE, whose agents undertook most of the more unpleasant aspects of counter-intelligence work. There were not many of them (a 1966 report gave only some 1,100 in Angola, as compared with 10,000 PSP and 10,000–20,000 OPVDCA), but they had a wide network of informers and their influence was considerable.

In general, the Portuguese were able to confine the guerrillas to border areas of relatively minor economic significance. In Angola they were helped by internal conflicts between the rival movements. In Guiné they lost ground initially (though no posts as such), but much of this was regained after 1968 by Spínola's determined and imaginative counter-offensive. Even in Moçambique the FRELIMO guerrillas made little headway in the centre and south until the very end of the war, though the opening of a second front in Tete Province certainly came as an unpleasant surprise to the Portuguese. In general, Portuguese casualties were tolerable, and the economic life of the provinces was not seriously affected. Angola, indeed, enjoyed an unprecedented economic boom during the 1960s. One American assessment said, 'The rebels cannot oust the Portuguese and the Portuguese can contain but not eliminate the rebels'.

The war imposed an immense and ever-increasing burden on Portugal itself, however; by the 1970s she was spending 40 per cent of her annual budget on the war effort. This strain was accompanied by an increasing degree of war-weariness among the troops. The national service period was increased to four years in 1967, and virtually all conscripts had to undertake a two-year tour in Africa. The proportion evading service (usually through emigration in search of better paid jobs in France) rose significantly. At the same time, the supply of officer candidates began to dry up. Applications for the Military Academy fell from 559 in 1961 to 155 in 1973. These developments were reflected in the attitudes of the non-élite metropolitan units who provided the static garrisons. They became reluctant to patrol, and complained that the settlers were letting them take all the risks while they relaxed in Luanda and Lorenço Marques.

The authorities reacted to the growing manpower crisis by trying to 'Africanise' the local forces. They did this by forming new 'spearhead' units recruited from the *Milícia* and largely trained by members of the OPVDC. These *Grupos Especiais* (GEs) first appeared in 1969. A *grupo* was equivalent to a combat group and consisted of one officer, nine NCOs and 18 soldiers. They were 90 per cent ethnically homogenous. From 1971 onwards the best of the recruits were incorporated into élite *Grupos Especiais Pára-quedistas* (GEPs), which were usually multi-ethnic. In addition, PIDE agents in both Angola and Moçambique organised groups of *Flechas* ('Arrows'). There is still a cloud of secrecy surrounding these latter units, and they remain little known; essentially, however, they were small groups of ex-guerrillas who carried Soviet pattern arms, wore guerrilla clothing and were employed on long range penetration activities (rather like the pseudo-gangs in Kenya or the Selous Scouts in Rhodesia). These three types of unit came under provincial rather than military control and were classified as *Forças Militarizadas* rather than *Forças Armados*. In practice, however, both the GEs and GEPs formed part of the *unidades de intervenção* along with the *pára-quedistas*, *fuzileiros* and *commandos*. By 1974 black troops outnumbered whites in all but Moçambique and Portugal itself, as the following table shows:

Casualty evacuation, Angola. This gives a good idea of the mixture of outfits worn by Air Force personnel in the 1960s. The machines in the background are Do-27s.

	Black	White	Total
Angola	37,000	24,200	61,200
Guiné	24,800	6,200	31,000
Moçambique	19,800	24,200	44,000
Portugal		60,000	60,000
Total	81,600	114,600	196,200

Most outside observers were taken by surprise by

the sudden and dramatic collapse of the Portuguese regime in April 1974, but in reality the coup had been brewing for some time. The immediate cause was a 1973 decree designed to persuade *miliciano* officers to become regulars by allowing them to count all their previous service towards seniority. Middle-ranking regulars were enraged at the prospect of being leap-frogged by conscript captains, and this provided much of the motive power behind the development of the *Movimento das Forças Armadas* (Armed Forces Movement or MFA), which was initially a kind of career officers' association.

Faced with government inflexibility, the MFA began to move towards the left; many of the younger regulars had begun to be recruited from relatively underprivileged backgrounds after Dr Salazar abolished tuition fees at the Military Academy in 1958, and others had been influenced by their Marxist opponents. At this point, Spínola (now a general and Deputy Chief of Staff) published a book entitled *Portugal e o Futuro*, which argued that the government should seek a political solution to the war before its strains led the country into revolutionary disintegration. Spínola had long been convinced that the war in Guiné was unwinnable, and had already tried unsuccessfully to persuade Dr Salazar's successor Dr Caetano to open negotiations with the PAIGC.

Caetano promptly dismissed Spínola, and tried to ban the circulation of his book in the overseas provinces. Indignation boiled over, and the MFA realised that a coup would be welcomed by most of the population. It duly took place on 25 April 1974. The MFA Committee then invited Spínola to take over as president. He hoped to negotiate a form of home rule for the overseas provinces within some kind of federal framework, but almost everyone else—including the officers, the *milicianos* and the civilians—wanted an end to the war. In July Spínola was forced to agree to negotiations over the transfer of power, and a few weeks later he resigned.

While this power struggle was going on in Lisbon, Portuguese units in the field simply retreated into their barracks, negotiating local ceasefires and ignoring official orders to continue fighting. They refused to support an abortive right wing settler revolt in Moçambique. Meanwhile, the increasingly left wing MFA junta negotiated independence

An F-84 over Luanda in the early 1960s. This aircraft was painted silver, with bright orange nose, tail and wing tanks.

treaties with Guiné's PAIGC and Moçambique's FRELIMO. It tried to negotiate an agreement with the warring Angolan factions as well, but this proved an impossible task; and in November 1975 Portugal's last African High Commissioner simply hauled down his country's flag and departed.

It was not quite the end, however, for many African-born Portuguese soldiers remained behind, especially in Angola. Some of the more radical elected to serve with the MPLA forces, while others fought on with the FNLA or UNITA, eventually ending up in South Africa's élite Portuguese-speaking 32 Battalion.

The Plates

A1: General, Tropical Dress Uniform, 1961
Most colonial armies had a white dress uniform for hot weather ceremonial purposes, and the Portuguese model did not differ very much from the British or the French patterns except that the cap was also all-white. Marshals had two rows of oak leaf embroidery on the peak, generals one, colonels a row of laurel leaf braid, and other officers plain 'chevron' braid, all in gold. This officer is Governor General of an Overseas Province and so has additional stars above those denoting his rank, which are gold instead of the usual silver. Other officers had dark blue epaulettes instead of red:

these colours were also used for the slides worn on service and combat dress uniforms. Arm of service was shown by the badge worn on the cap band: no collar devices were worn with this uniform, but the gold buttons bore branch insignia. Generals and Staff had the five castles from the Portuguese arms within a wreath, and other arms wore a version of their normal cap badge. This uniform was worn by officers only and remains regulation to date, along with the bluish-grey metropolitan service dress.

A2: *Tenente Coronel, Air Force, 1961*

The Portuguese Air Force became a separate arm in 1925, but it retained army ranks and uniforms until 1966. The distinguishing device was a spread-winged eagle very similar to that of the Royal Air Force. This was worn on the cap and tunic collar, with the national coat of arms above on the officers' peaked caps. Army uniform was worn in Portugal itself, but the Air Force introduced its own distinctive tropical uniform in 1950, and this was generally worn in the African provinces. The beltless tunic was noticeably 'American' in style. The officers' version usually lacked shoulder straps, but narrow metallic ones were added in full dress. The men's version did have straps, on which were worn dark blue slides bearing silver or light blue chevrons (the Air Force had no rank below corporal). Undress consisted of the light khaki shirt and slacks or shorts, worn with a sidecap or peaked cap. This outfit was often worn in preference to flying clothing by the pilots of the light 'spotter' aircraft or helicopters. Field dress followed the army pattern. The Air Police formed during the 1960s to guard the airfields wore light blue berets with a badge consisting of the Portuguese arms surmounted by the winged eagle.

A3: *Segundo Cabo, Infantry, 1960*

This uniform dated from 1948, but it was essentially the same as that worn by the *caçadores indígena* from the early years of the century. The main difference was that boots and canvas gaiters had replaced the earlier khaki puttees and bare feet. The gaiters were replaced by knee-length khaki stockings and ankle boots in Guiné. The *cofia* (fez) had originally borne a company number in brass, sometimes over the 'armillary sphere' which formed part of the Portuguese arms and which had been adopted as the badge of the colonial troops, but these were not worn during the 1950s. European ranks were supposed to wear a tropical helmet, tunic and long trousers with spat-type gaiters, but more commonly wore a slouch hat, khaki bush jacket, shorts and long stockings instead, and paraded in steel helmets. The undress headdress common to soldiers of both races was a plain sidecap bearing the arm-of-service badge in brass. This NCO's m/937 Mauser is identical with the standard German 98k, but his leather equipment is of Portuguese origin. This 'colonial' uniform quickly became obsolete, except for Bands and 'Fanfares', which retained it until about 1967.

Portuguese combat uniforms. These sketches are based on the official Portuguese drawings, but there were many variations in practice. The 2A/2B was khaki, the others made in French camouflage pattern material. The *dolman* (combat jacket) was worn far more frequently than the shirt. The press studs around the collar were for a detachable hood (seldom worn in practice and not illustrated here). Note that the *para-quedistas* generally wore the French airborne troops' 1947/56 combat dress, which resembled the 2-C but had a small additional pocket superimposed on the left breast pocket, and pleated trouser pockets (a number also used the 1947/52 trousers, which had additional small pockets on the fronts of the upper thighs).

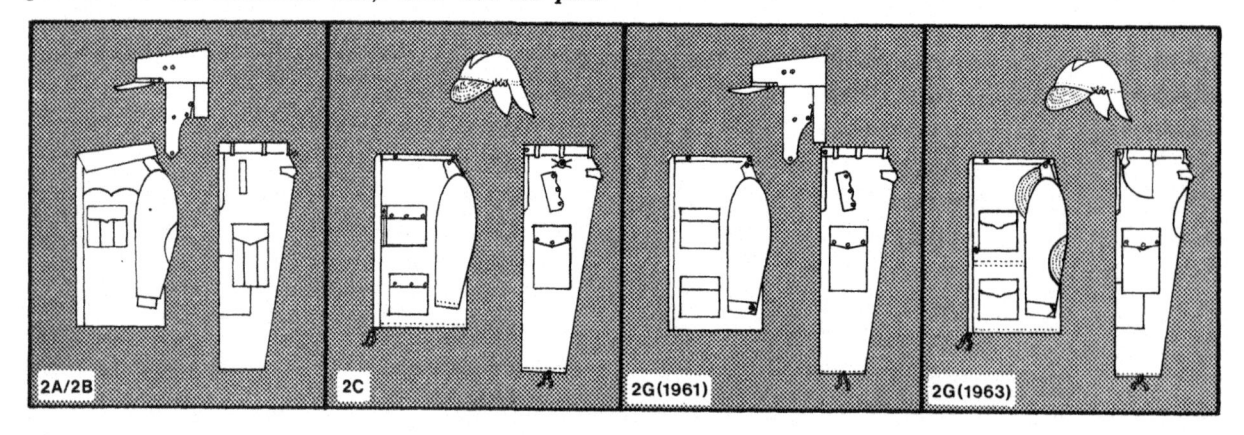

2A/2B 2C 2G(1961) 2G(1963)

36

A North American F-86G on the ground during the mid-1960s. This machine was mostly white, with a plain metal fin and black nose and number.

B1: General, Overseas Service Dress, 1961

This general wears the new overseas campaign uniform introduced in 1960 for all troops other than *caçadores*. There were two versions, one for the hot season and the other for the cooler periods. The first (Model 2-A) was made of light cotton and the second (Model 2-B) of a terylene and wool mixture. There was also a blue-grey version for use in Portugal itself but this was not worn overseas, though the grey home service pattern greatcoat could be (this was single breasted, with patch breast pockets for all ranks down to sergeant). The jacket, known as a *camisa dolman*, could be worn with the collar open or closed, but the style shown here was usually restricted to walking out dress for other ranks. The field cap had a neck curtain and separate ear flaps which could be fastened under the chin. An olive khaki web belt was usually worn as part of field dress. Many troops continued to wear the older ankle boots and canvas spat gaiters with this uniform. Insignia was kept to a minimum and consisted of metal arm-of-service badges worn on the cap and collar, with ranks being shown on shoulder strap slides.

B2: Soldado, Infantry Field Dress, 1961

The troops sent out to Angola in 1961 arrived wearing the 1960 field cap and *camisa dolman*, but most photographs show them campaigning in the No. 2 pattern shirt designed to be worn beneath the *dolman*, and with the field cap replaced by the distinctive Portuguese steel helmet first adopted in 1940. At this period only the *pára-quedistas* and *caçadores* had camouflaged uniforms and the helmet usually lacked any form of cover. It was rarely worn after the initial campaigns. Almost all the men of the expeditionary force seem to have received the new 1960 pattern combat boots with their integral leather anklets. In walking-out dress the field cap or helmet was replaced by a sidecap bearing the arm-of-service badge, the web belt by a cloth one and the field trousers by plain ones. Other ranks still wore these with boots and gaiters, but sergeants and above were permitted long trousers and plain black shoes. Alternatively, troops could wear shorts and long khaki stockings. The weapon is the Portuguese-designed and produced FPB m/948, a fairly conventional sub-machine gun with a fitting for a short knife bayonet.

B3: Cabo, Caçadores, Combat Dress, 1961

The *caçadores* were the only army troops to wear a camouflaged field uniform. This was the 1960 Model 2-C. Both the style and the material were clearly modelled on the French pattern. The *dolman* (combat jacket) was very similar to the French paratroops' *veste de saute mle 1947/56*, even to the small vertical zipped opening on the inner side of the left breast pocket. The khaki No. 2 shirt was

37

A Fiat G91 in the early 1970s, displaying late war pattern green and grey camouflage, with the national insignia reduced to narrow red-before-green stripes at the base of the fin.

supposed to be worn underneath, but it was frequently omitted in the tropics. The trousers had twin thigh pockets, and the cap resembled the French *'casquette Bigeard'*. Rank slides (green chevrons on blue for *caçadores*) were worn with this uniform, but no arm-of-service insignia. In walking-out order *caçadores* wore the same khaki *camisa dolman* as the remainder of the army. Instead of the sidecap, however, they were given a chestnut brown *boina* or beret with red and green ribbons at the back. This NCO carries the Dutch-manufactured 7.92mm AR-10, a little known predecessor of the M-16: the Portuguese purchased a consignment of these in 1959–60. Most went to the *pára-quedistas* and Air Police, but some reached other units of the expeditionary force.

C1: Nurse, Combat Dress, 1961
In August 1961 it was decided to extend the use of the camouflaged combat uniform to all arms, reportedly because the guerrillas were singling out the *caçadores*. The khaki 1960 pattern 2-A and 2-B campaign uniforms were accordingly abolished. The camouflaged uniform was redesigned and designated Model 2-G. The *dolman* differed from the 2-C pattern in that the pockets had concealed fastenings, the cuffs had buttoned tabs and the lower hem had no drawstring fastening, these details again resembling the equivalent French 'all arms' camouflage clothing. Like the earlier model it had a plain round collar and a detachable hood. The arrangement of the trouser side pockets was also simplified, though the thigh pockets were retained. The new 2-G field cap was a camouflaged version of the 1960 2-A/B pattern, with the same neck and ear flaps. Photographs show that it was quite widely worn in the early 1960s, but the 2-C cap was retained as an alternative and seems to have been more popular with the troops. The shoulder strap slides remained dark blue, with Infantry, Artillery, Cavalry and Engineer corporals having red chevrons, Medical crimson, and Administration light blue. This nurse is one of a number who served in the front lines alongside the 'men in green'.

C2: Capitão, Cavalry, 1961
When the use of camouflaged combat dress was extended to all arms in 1961, the khaki *camisa dolman* was modified and restricted to walking-out. The new model retained the 'Sahariano'-style shoulders but added skirt pockets and an integral cloth belt. All ranks were authorised to wear the plain trousers and shoes previously reserved for sergeants and above. The sidecap was replaced by the beret for all arms. The regulation colour was chestnut brown (this shade had considerable prestige in Portugal, having been associated with the élite *caçadores* since the Peninsular War), but Artillery, Cavalry, Signals, Supply, Medical, Ordnance and General Service were authorised to wear black ones as a temporary measure. Ribbons were supposed to be worn at the back in arm-of-service colours: Generals

red, Staff mid-blue, Infantry (including *caçadores*) red and green, Artillery red and black, Cavalry red and yellow, Engineers green and black, Signals black, Supply light blue, Medical crimson, Ordnance brick colour, and General Service green and yellow. In practice this regulation was seldom observed, and most troops wore the Infantry's green and red. The badge on the left breast indicated completion of the armoured car course.

C3: Soldado, Signals, Working Dress, 1963
In hot weather both the long trousers and the *camisa dolman* were too constricting, and it was normal for all ranks to wear khaki shirts and shorts. The shirt was the standard No. 2 and the shorts were worn with long stockings. The canvas 'baseball boots' shown here replaced a lighter model of 'tennis shoe' after 1961. The old fashioned side- or 'bivouac' cap remained in use for fatigue duties until 1966, but the shirt and shorts could also be worn with the beret for hot weather walking-out dress. Military Police were not allowed to wear shorts on duty: they had white helmets with a black band and 'PM' on the front, and dark blue brassards bearing the same letters in white.

D1: Subtenente, Fuzileiros, Combat Dress, 1964
Further modifications were made to combat dress in December 1963. The khaki shirt was replaced by a similar pattern in camouflaged material, designated 2-G, which allowed troops to fight in shirtsleeve order. The *dolman* was modified by the removal of the cuff tabs, the re-adoption of the drawstring, the re-shaping of the pocket flaps to give a slightly pointed appearance, and the addition of semi-circular reinforcing patches on the elbows and shoulders. The trousers received a similar reinforcement on the seat. Camouflaged rank slides replaced dark blue ones in the field. This modified uniform was known as the 2-G m963. Commanding officers were allowed to authorise it for walking-out, sentry duty and guards of honour, in which case it was supposed to be worn with the corps beret, white gloves and dark blue rank slides. The *fuzileiros* formed part of the Navy, and although they wore standard combat dress they were distinguished by a black beret with anchor badge and the use of Naval rank insignia (ratings wore the same chevrons as Army NCOs). In parade order they wore white Navy pattern uniforms with black berets and combat boots. The white uniform for ratings and junior NCOs was similar to the British seamen's pattern, while that worn by senior NCOs and officers consisted of a single-breasted high collar tunic and trousers. This junior officer carries the standard Walther P1 pistol.

D2: Primeiro Cabo, Engineers, Work Uniform, 1966
A final simplification of the uniforms took place in 1966. The 2-G m963 camouflaged combat dress remained unchanged, but the khaki walking-out uniform was abolished and replaced by new olive green service dress (No. 2) and work uniforms (No. 3). The new No. 2 shirt had patch pockets and either long or short sleeves. The normal headdress remained the beret, but officers were authorised a green peaked cap with black peak and gold cord and insignia. The No. 3 work uniform shown here had a plain green version of the standard 2-C field cap, a simplified shirt with plain cuffs and patch pockets, and trousers which retained the combat uniform's useful thigh pockets. It was occasionally worn as field dress. 1966 also saw the introducion of new lace-up combat boots to replace the older cuffed pattern. The shoulder strap slides were changed to olive green, and the junior NCOs' chevrons to plain red for all arms. This also applied to the camouflaged slides worn with the 2-G. In practice, few troops actually wore rank insignia in the field, and the only means of identification was

Seamen manning a quick-firing gun on patrol. This picture shows the distinctive shape of the Portuguese steel helmet, worn by all arms other than paratroops.

Fuzileiros on parade, wearing white seamen's vests and trousers with black berets and combat boots. The berets' green and red ribbons can be clearly seen.

the tag hung on a cord around the neck. These changes took some time to introduce, and older patterns of uniform and insignia remained in use until 1974. This Engineer NCO is examining a *pica*, that simple but effective anti-mine detector widely used to probe dirt roads.

D3: Segundo Sargento, Artillery, Service Dress, 1966

The battledress *bluse* shown here was first introduced in 1960 as a cold weather alternative to the *camisa dolman*. It appeared in both blue-grey (metropolitan Portugal) and khaki (overseas). It was modelled on the French army's '*blouson sportif*'. In 1966 the colours were changed to olive khaki for home use and olive green overseas. The domed buttons bore the five shields of the Portuguese coat of arms and were generally of a brownish shade. After 1966 this became normal winter service dress for all ranks except officers, who retained the older blue-grey service dress. In summer the same beret and slacks were worn with the shirt and tie. The 'temporary' black berets disappeared after 1963 and all arms wore the *caçadores*' brown with their own branch badge. There was a good deal of re-badging: a typical recruit would begin by wearing the Infantry badge of his parent regiment, then exchange this for the bugle device of the *caçadores* when he went to Africa. Specialists wore the badge of the branch to which they were attached on the beret, and their own branch badge on the collar.

E1: Capitão, Commandos, 1970

Uniforms did not change significantly after 1966, but various modifications crept in. The original 'French' camouflage pattern had green and brown patches on a light green base: this was changed during the 1960s to a mixture of dark, medium and light greens more suitable to the thick bush of Guiné and Moçambique, though the older pattern also remained in service until the end of the war. This officer wears the later 'green' pattern. At this period the only official distinction for the *commandos* was the arm-of-service badge worn on the universal brown beret, but his coloured cravat and metal shoulder title are typical of a whole series of 'unofficial' distinctions which became common in the later 1960s. The titles usually had gilt lettering on black, and sometimes indicated service in a particular theatre, e.g. 'GUINE'. The most common of these distinctions was the unit shield, enamelled on metal and usually (though not invariably) worn on the left breast. The practice developed whereby each battalion, squadron or independent company had its own *cresca*: as a result there were literally thousands of separate designs. This officer wears the shield later adopted (with a crimson beret) by the Commando Regiment.

E2: Soldado, Dragoons, Field Dress, 1972

The *dragões* wore the standard service dress with either a field cap or brown beret, the latter bearing the Cavalry's crossed swords. The cavalry tradition was strong in the Portuguese army, however, and most had either riding boots or leggings. The use of the camouflaged shirt in place of the *dolman* had become increasingly common. It was noticeable that what might be called 'protective' equipment was lacking by comparison with the US troops in Vietnam at the same period. The steel helmet was hardly ever used, and there were no flak jackets. Equipment was lightened as much as possible. The standard web equipment had shoulder braces, for instance, but these were invariably discarded and soldiers normally carried no more than a couple of ammunition pouches and a water bottle. By the mid-1960s the sturdy and reliable G-3 rifle had become almost universal. The *dragões* carried the retractable-stock version, together with Walther P1 pistols.

E3: Warrant Officer, Paratroops, 1974
The *Boinas Verdes* ('Green Berets') generally wore black front-lacing jump boots with one of the various models of the French paratroops' *'tenue de saut'*. The *dolman*, often abbreviated after the fashion of French élite units, is worn here with a decorative belt clasp bearing the *pára-quedistas'* crest. The epaulette slides were dark blue with either silver (officers and senior NCOs) or light blue (junior NCOs) rank insignia. French 'OTAN' pattern steel helmets were worn in 1959, but by 1961 these had been replaced by the US paratroop model, normally worn plain or with a net cover. The *pára-quedistas'* overseas service dress originally consisted of the Air Force's light khaki tunic and slacks, worn with the green *boina* bearing a gilt badge consisting of a parachute superimposed on crossed rifles. This was adopted in 1956 and marked the beret's first appearance in Portuguese service. In 1966 the whole Air Force adopted a mid-blue uniform with silver buttons, similar in style to the earlier tropical khaki model. The paratroops retained their green berets, but adopted the Air Force's silver eagle within a gilt wreath. By the mid-1960s they had exchanged their unusual AR-10 rifles for the univeral G-3s (generally the retractable-stock model).

F1: Volunteer, OPVDCA, 1970
The original settler volunteers had no uniforms. Photographs show the majority of them to have been barehead and dressed in white shirts and khaki trousers. Most seem to have carried the regulation Mauser rifle. The first move towards uniformity came after the formation of the OPVDC with the issue of an armband in the national colours of red and green and bearing the organisation's badge in white. This depicted a crossed cutlass and plough beneath interlaced initials 'O' and 'V'. The situation was regularised during the later 1960s with the issue of standard olive green 1966 pattern No. 2 uniforms. The service uniform consisted of a plain field cap, long-sleeved shirt, trousers, web belt and canvas boots. The parade or walking-out uniform shown here substituted a black beret, a short-sleeved shirt, white neckerchief and black boots, with the OPVDC badge on the beret and left breast. There seems to have been no special form of rank insignia, and NCOs presumably wore green epaulette slides bearing either silver or red chevrons. The OPVDC became increasingly multi-racial during the early 1970s, but remained the main vehicle for mobilising the white settler population.

A *fuzileiro* on patrol in Guiné, carrying the G-3. The beret bears a plain anchor badge.

F2: Volunteer, Grupos Especiais, 1972
The GEs and the GEPs were not army formations, although they came under military operational control after command was unified in 1970, and they had their own distinctive black uniform. This was similar to the 1966 fatigue dress in general outline, but the field service cap was based on the 1961 2-G pattern, with combined neck and ear flaps which were usually fastened up over the crown. According to regulations the shirt had plain pockets and the trousers were plain, but photographs show that most uniforms actually had pleated breast and thigh pockets. The field service dress included an olive green web belt and canvas boots. Coloured berets, neckerchiefs and boot laces were worn in walking-out order, with the addition of white gloves for parades. Each *Grupo* had its own colour: e.g. GE 218 light blue, GE 220 red, GE 225 yellow, and GE 230 white. The GEPs appear to have favoured yellow berets. The regulations did not prescribe any particular badges or other devices, but photographs

Fuzileiros launching inflatable boats. Guiné was a maze of waterways, and the *fuzilieiros*' amphibious expertise was particularly useful there.

suggest that these troops commonly wore the Commando beret badge, and had their own unit shields. The 'parade rest' position demonstrated by this volunteer was adopted after the introduction of the G-3 and was peculiar to the Portuguese forces.

F3: Primeiro Sargento, Police/Milícia, 1973
The Police NCOs in command of *Milícia* platoons continued to wear their own uniforms. This field version was introduced during the mid-1960s. The jacket was based on the Army's 1961 pattern *camisa dolman*, but incorporated some of the features introduced in the 1963 pattern combat dress, such as the ribbed reinforcement patches on the shoulders and elbows, the practical thigh pockets and the extra reinforcements at the knee. The cap was a modernised version of the 'kepi' worn by the Police at the start of the war. The silver badge consisted of the interlaced letters 'P' and 'S' within a six-pointed star surrounded by a wreath, and the rank bars or chevrons were silver on black for all ranks. Ordinary militiamen wore the 1966 model No. 3 work uniform, with a web belt, canvas boots and either long trousers or shorts. Ordinary militia

usually carried obsolete Mauser rifles, but this senior NCO is equipped with the UZI SMG, numbers of which were bought during the 1960s.

G1: Angola: FNLA 'regular', 1964

Holden Roberto's 'exterior' FNLA was given training facilities in Congo-Kinshasa (later Zaire) and received both clothing and equipment from a sympathetic President Mobuto. This Bakongo soldier is actually wearing a 1961 pattern ANC (Congolese Army) uniform and carries a post-war .30 cal. Belgian FN Mauser rifle donated by the ANC. The FNLA officers of the period were equally smartly turned out in US-style combat jackets and stiffened field caps, though like most guerrilla forces they wore no insignia. This parade ground smartness was maintained right up to 1974, when the FNLA troops appeared in new green field caps and fatigues. By then their ex-Congolese weapons had been replaced by Chinese Type 56 copies of the SKS carbine or AK-47. However, smartness did not equal combat effectiveness, and the FNLA was soundly defeated in the civil war which followed the Portuguese withdrawal, despite the intervention of Zairean infantry and armoured cars (together with some ill-fated British mercenaries).

G2: Angola: MPLA guerrilla, 1970

The MPLA were on the whole less well equipped than the FNLA, and their FAPLA troops wore a mixture of civilian and military-style clothing. Some certainly had the frequently encountered 'rain drop' pattern cap, shirt and trousers, while others wore captured Portuguese uniforms, but most remained ragged in the extreme. MPLA and UNITA units operating in the plateau areas of Angola felt the cold acutely, and overcoats of various types were not uncommon. This unusually well-equipped bodyguard wears a loose hooded top made from the older, 1960s pattern Soviet camouflaged material and anonymous olive green trousers. His visored field cap is similar to that worn by almost all the liberation movements: it appeared in a variety of colours and materials. He carries the widely used SKS carbine.

G3: Angola: UNITA guerrilla, 1974

UNITA's FALA was probably the least well-equipped of all the main guerrilla movements, and

Portuguese Rank Insignia: (1) *Marechal* (gold stars) or *Chefe Do Estado Maior Do Exército* (silver stars) **(2)** *General* **(3)** *Brigadeiro* **(4)** *Coronel Tirocinado* (Probationer Colonel) **(5)** *Coronel* **(6)** *Tenente Coronel* **(7)** *Major* **(8)** *Capitão Tirocinado* (Probationer Captain) **(9)** *Capitão* **(10)** *Tenente* **(11)** *Alferes* **(12)** *Sargento Ajudante* **(13)** *1° Sargento* **(14)** *2° Sargento* **(15)** *Furriel* **(16)** *1° Cabo* (with promotion approved to next rank) **(17)** *1° Cabo* **(18)** *2° Cabo* **(19)** *Soldado Arvorado*.

Insignia were silver on red for Nos. 2–3, gold on dark blue for Nos. 4–15, and arm-of-service colour (see plate notes) on dark blue for Nos. 16–19. On field dress insignia were to be grey (*marechals* yellow) on uniform colour slides, though coloured devices were frequently worn in practice. An Army officer acting as Governor of an Overseas Province wore two additional six-pointed gold stars above his normal insignia, and a Governor-General three such stars. An Army officer acting as Under-secretary to the Army Ministry wore five silver five-pointed stars, as Army Minister five gold stars, as Minister of Defence six silver stars and as President of the Republic six gold stars.

Militia on parade. They carry obsolete Mauser rifles and wear 1966 pattern work dress. The armband is red over green with a metal unit shield. The two officers wear olive green 1966 pattern service dress, one with a brown beret, the other with a green peaked cap.

was hard put to find weapons, let alone clothing. However, this unit commander is reasonably well turned out with a typically mixed collection of items: captured Portuguese trousers and canvas boots, a military pattern shirt of unknown origin, and a green beret sporting one of the party badges frequently worn by militants of all movements. UNITA's bore its distinctive *galo negro* (black cock) and red sun on a green map of Angola; the FNLA badge was a white disc with a yellow edged red diagonal band bearing a yellow star; and the MPLA's was a yellow star on a disc divided horizontally red over black. Many UNITA commanders adopted Portuguese-style rank insignia, though apparently only in the final year of the war.

H1: Guiné: PAIGC 'regular', 1974
Although the PAIGC's forces came closest to being a conventional army, they did not adopt standard uniforms or insignia. Most guerrillas wore a mixture of civilian or work clothing, khaki or olive green fatigues or ex-Portuguese combat uniforms of various patterns. One PAIGC combatant even managed to acquire the gilt and red parade cockade from a Russian peaked cap and mount it on his black beret. However, field caps, shirts and field trousers manufactured from East German 'rain drop' pattern cloth became common during the later 1960s, and also seem to have equipped many of the more 'regular' Marxist units in Angola and Moçambique as well. It was usually worn with a plain field cap, but 'rain drop' berets were also to be seen; and PAIGC 'regulars' (especially artillery and heavy weapons crews) sometimes wore the East German steel helmet illustrated here, which was almost always left in its original stone grey shade. Personal equipment was usually restricted to a waist belt and ammunition pouch.

Black members of the OPVDCA on parade in the early 1970s. The parade uniform had a black beret and white neck scarf. The banner was red and green with a white badge. The men in the background carry FNs, many of which were purchased in the early 1960s but which later became 'limited standard'.

Portuguese Branch Insignia (all gold and worn on beret and collar unless otherwise noted): (1) Generals and Staff, cap (2) officers, cap (3) Air Force to 1966, cap (4) Air Force to 1966, beret; gold eagle, silver surround, full colour shield. (5) Generals, collar (6) Staff, collar (7) Paratroops, beret to 1966 (8) Air Force, cap and beret post-1966; silver eagle, gold wreath. (9) Infantry, cap (10) Infantry (11) MGs, cap (12) *Caçadores* (13) Artillery, cap and beret (14) Artillery, collar (15) Cavalry, silver on beret (16) Lancers (17) Engineers (18) Telegraphists (19) Technical (20) Cryptographers (21) Doctors (22) Medical NCOs (23) Supply (24) Clerks (25) Veterinary (26) Transport (27) Postal (28) Chaplains (29) Commandos (30) *Policia*, silver, cap (31) OPVDCA, white, beret and chest (32) *Fuzileiros*' beret. Specialists attached to line units wore the unit's badge on cap or beret, their own badge on the collar.

45

Members of a Moçambique *Grupo Especiais* on parade c.1974. Note the coloured berets, scarves and bootlaces. Apart from their beret badges and pocket shields, the men appear to be wearing a local pattern of rank insignia in the form of small bars at the top of the sleeve rather than chevrons on the straps.

H2: Moçambique: FRELIMO *guerrilla*, 1970

This combatant wears a typically nondescript khaki field cap and shirt, but his trousers are made from standard green and buff Soviet camouflage material. Other photographs show FRELIMO troops wearing hooded smocks made of the same material. Soviet camouflage suits usually took the form of overalls but these were probably too hot for the climate, though it is not clear whether the two-piece versions were delivered as such or made up locally. The cap was sometimes camouflaged with a plaited grass ring into which were stuck standing stalks a foot or so high. He carries the drum-fed RPD machine gun with a couple of spare drums in the haversack on his left hip. He has a light rucksack, but carries his water supply in a commercial thermos (hardly any guerrillas seem to have had water bottles).

H3: Moçambique: FRELIMO *'regular'*, 1974

FRELIMO detachments at the independence ceremonies wore 'rain drop' caps, shirts and trousers, but many of the movement's 'regulars' wore this khaki uniform during the later stages of the conflict. It was also used by the MPLA in Angola, equipping many of its troops during the civil war which followed the Portuguese withdrawal and becoming the standard dress of the Angolan Militia afterwards. (It was also used by some of the Rhodesian Patriotic Front guerrillas.) The simple and practical 'sun hat' was undoubtedly of Soviet origin, but equipment came from a variety of sources. 'ChiCom'-style chest pouches were widely used, and some troops even received the newly designed Bulgarian M72 steel helmet. This soldier is unusually well outfitted with a modern rucksack: he carries a Chinese-made (Type 56) copy of the RPG rocket launcher, one of the guerrillas' most important weapons.

INDEX

Figures in **bold** refer to illustrations.

'Agostinho Neto Trail' 9
Air Force, Portuguese **20**, 20–1, 24, **34**, **35**, **37**, **38**
Angola 8–11, **34**
  uniforms 43, **G**

branch insignia, Portuguese **45**

Cabral, Amilcar 8, 11, 13
Caetano, Dr 11
Chipenda, Daniel 10
Commando Training School, Lamego 24
CONCP 8
COREMO 14
counter-intelligence 33

Dahomey, independence of 7

ELNA 9
EPLA 9

FARP 12, 13
FLING 11
FNLA 8, 9, 10, 44
  uniforms 43, **G**
FPLM 14–16
FRELIMO 8, 13–16, **34**
  uniforms 46, **H**

Grupos Especiais (GEs) **34**, **F**
  uniforms 42, 46
Guevara, Che 10
Guiné 11–13
  uniforms **H**

'hearts and minds' campaigns 33
Henry the Navigator 4

Kaunda, President 10

Liberation Movements 7–16

Machel, Samora 14, 15
'Maria's War' 21
Military Police **9**, 16, 33
  uniforms 42–3, **F**
Mobuto, President 9–10
Mondlane, Eduardo 8, 13–14, 15
Mozambique 13–16
  uniforms **H**
MPLA 8, 9–10, 11, 44
  uniforms 43, **G**

NATO 16
Navy, Portuguese 24–33
Neto, Dr Angostinho 8, 10
Nyerere, President Julius 10, 13

Operation 'Gordian Knot' 15
OPVDCA 33, 34, **F**
  uniforms 41, **45**
overseas forces, Portuguese, organisation of 19–22

PAIGC 8, 11–13
  uniforms 44, **H**
paratroops 21, **21**
PIDE 4, 8, 33
'Pidjiguiti Massacre' 12
Portugal's African Empire 4–7
Portuguese Forces **14**, 16–35, **18**
  in action 23–35, **24**
  Air Force **20**, 20–1, 24, **34**, **35**, **37**, **38**
  branch insignia **45**
  military vehicles **11**, 18–19, **33**
  mine clearance 15
  Navy, the 24, 33
  overseas forces, organisation of 19–22
  paratroops 21, **21**
  rank insignia **43**
  Special Forces 24

uniforms **4**, **6**, **8**, **9**, **10**, **12**, **15**, **34**, 35–43, **36**, **40**, **44**, **A**, **B**, **C**, **D**, **E**
unit organisation 16–17, **17**
unit shields 19
weapons **6**, **13**, **16**, 17–18, **39**, **41**

rank insignia, Portuguese **43**
Roberto, Holden 8, 9

Salazar, Dr 4, 6, 7, 16
Savimbi, Jonas 10
Spanish Civil War 16
Special Units 24
Spínola, Brig. 13, 34

uniforms
  FNLA 43, **G**
  FRELIMO 46, **H**
  Grupos Especiais (GE) 42, 46, **F**
  Military Police 42–3, **F**
  MPLA 43, **G**
  OPVDCA 41, **45**, **F**
  PAIGC 44, **H**
  Portuguese Forces **4**, **6**, **8**, **9**, **10**, **12**, **15**, **34**, 35–43, **36**, **40**, **44**, **A**, **B**, **C**, **D**, **E**
  UNITA 43–4, **G**
UNITA 10, 11
  uniforms 43–4, **G**
UPA 8, 9, 21

Victor, Geraldo 6

weapons
  ELNA (Angola) 9
  FARP (Guiné) 12, 13
  FPLM (Mozambique) 14–15
  Portuguese Forces **6**, **13**, **16**, 17–18, **39**, **41**
World War I 16, 21